WHAT IS THE BOOK OF HEBREWS?

Kids' Guides to God's Word Series

What Is the Book of Genesis?
What Is the Book of Exodus?
What Is the Book of Leviticus?
What Is the Book of Numbers?
What Is the Book of Deuteronomy?
What Is the Book of Joshua?
What Is the Book of Judges?
What Is the Book of Ruth?
What Is the Book of 1 Samuel?
What Is the Book of 2 Samuel?
What Is the Book of 1 Kings?
What Is the Book of 2 Kings?
What Are the Books of 1–2 Chronicles?
What Are the Books of Ezra & Nehemiah?
What Is the Book of Esther?
What Is the Book of Job?
What Is the Book of Psalms?
What Is the Book of Proverbs?
What Is the Book of Ecclesiastes?
What Are the Books of Song of Songs & Lamentations?
What Is the Book of Isaiah?
What Is the Book of Jeremiah?
What Is the Book of Ezekiel?
What Is the Book of Daniel?
What Are the Books of Hosea–Micah?
What Are the Books of Nahum–Malachi?
What Is the Gospel of Matthew?
What Is the Gospel of Mark?
What Is the Gospel of Luke?
What Is the Gospel of John?
What Is the Book of Acts?
What Is the Book of Romans?
What Is the Book of 1 Corinthians?
What Is the Book of 2 Corinthians?
What Is the Book of Galatians?
What Is the Book of Ephesians?
What Is the Book of Philippians?
What Are the Books of Colossians & Philemon?
What Are the Books of 1–2 Thessalonians?
What Are the Books of 1–2 Timothy & Titus?
What Is the Book of Hebrews?
What Is the Book of James?
What Are the Books of 1–2 Peter & Jude?
What Are the Books of 1-3 John?
What Is the Book of Revelation?

What Is the Book of

HEBREWS?

Michael Whitworth

ISBN 978-1-971767-21-5

Published by Start2Finish
Bend, Oregon 97702
start2finish.org

Printed in the United States of America

30 29 28 27 26 1 2 3 4 5

CONTENTS

INTRODUCTION

Have you ever wanted to quit something that mattered? Not something small, like a boring video game or a book that wasn't very good. Something important. Something you believed in. Maybe you were part of a team that kept losing, and every practice felt pointless. Maybe you were trying to do the right thing at school, but the kids who cut corners seemed to be doing better than you. Maybe you were holding on to your faith, but life got hard enough that you started wondering if it was worth it.

That's where the first readers of Hebrews were. They were Jewish people who had come to believe that Jesus was the Messiah, the promised King their nation had been waiting for. And it had cost them. Their families thought they were traitors. Their communities pushed them out. Some of them had been publicly humiliated. Some had their property seized. Some had friends thrown in prison.

For a while, they endured it. The faith was new and exciting, and the cost felt worth paying. But time passed. Jesus didn't return as quickly as they expected. The pressure didn't let up. And now they were tired. Worn out. Starting to wonder if they'd made a mistake.

It would have been easy to go back. Judaism was legal in the Roman Empire. It was respected. It had a long history, a beautiful temple, an established priesthood, and centuries of tradition. Christianity had none of those things. Walking back into the synagogue would mean walking away from Jesus, but it would also mean walking away from the shame, the losses, and the loneliness.

Some of them were already drifting.

That's when someone sat down and wrote the most extraordinary sermon in the New Testament.

We don't know who wrote Hebrews. That might seem strange, but it's true. The author never identifies himself. People have guessed Paul, Barnabas, Apollos, Luke, and others, but nobody knows for certain. For my money, I think it was Timothy, but I can't prove it. What we do know is that the author was brilliant, deeply trained in the Old Testament, and passionately concerned about a group of believers who were in danger of throwing away everything they had gained.

And the argument this author made is unlike anything else in Scripture.

Most of the New Testament talks about what Jesus did: his life, his teaching, his miracles, his death, his resurrection. Hebrews talks about what Jesus is *right now*. This very moment. It tells us that the risen Jesus isn't just sitting in heaven waiting for history to end. He's actively working as our High Priest, representing his people before the Father, providing grace for every temptation, sustaining everyone who trusts him. He offered one sacrifice for sin, once for all, and then sat down at the right hand of God, where he intercedes for his people and will never, ever stop.

That's the argument of Hebrews: you can't go back, because there's nothing to go back to. The old system of priests and sacrifices and tabernacles was never the real thing. It was a shadow. A preview. A copy of something far greater that has now arrived in Jesus. Going back to the shadow when the reality has come would be like choosing a photograph of your family over your actual family. It makes no sense.

But Hebrews doesn't just argue. It warns. Again and again, the author pauses his theology to issue some of the most urgent warnings in the Bible. Don't drift. Don't harden your heart. Don't fall away. Don't throw away your confidence. Don't shrink back. The author loves these people, and he's terrified that some of them are going to let go of the only thing that can save them.

And then, right alongside those warnings, he pours out encouragement. You have an anchor for your soul. You have a priest who understands your weakness. You have access to the throne of grace. You have a better covenant, a better sacrifice, a better hope. You are surrounded by a great cloud of witnesses. Jesus himself is the pioneer and perfecter of your faith, and he has already crossed the finish line.

Warning and encouragement, warning and encouragement. That's the rhythm of Hebrews. Like a parent grabbing a child's shoulders and saying, "Listen to me. This is dangerous. But you can make it. Don't give up."

Here's a roadmap of where we're headed.

Chapter 1 introduces the Son of God in the most exalted

terms the Bible has to offer. He is the radiance of God's glory, the creator of the universe, the one who sustains all things by his powerful word. And he is greater than the angels.

Chapter 2 shows that this same exalted Son became human. He took on flesh and blood so he could die for us, destroy the power of death, and become our merciful High Priest.

Chapter 3 compares Jesus with Moses and then plunges into the story of the wilderness generation, the Israelites who saw God's miracles but refused to trust him. Their failure is a warning: don't let the same thing happen to you.

Chapter 4 reveals Jesus as a High Priest who sympathizes with our weakness because he was tempted in every way we are, yet without sin. Because of him, we can approach God's throne with confidence.

Chapter 5 confronts the readers for their spiritual laziness and warns them about the terrifying possibility of falling away from the faith completely.

Chapter 6 unpacks the mysterious figure of Melchizedek and shows that Jesus' priesthood is not like the old Levitical system. It is older, greater, and permanent. He saves completely, and he never stops interceding.

Chapter 7 takes us inside the heavenly sanctuary. This is the theological heart of the letter, where the author explains the new covenant, the once-for-all sacrifice, and the staggering truth that God will remember our sins no more.

Chapter 8 answers the question "Now what?" with three commands: draw near to God, hold fast to hope, and take care of each other. It also issues the letter's most severe warning about the consequences of rejecting Christ.

Chapter 9 walks through the great hall of faith, a parade of witnesses from Abel to the unnamed martyrs who lived and died trusting God's promises.

Chapter 10 brings the letter to its climax with the image of a race, the discipline of a loving Father, the contrast between the terror of Sinai and the joy of the heavenly Jerusalem, and a vision of an unshakable kingdom that will outlast the universe.

Why should you care about a letter written two thousand years ago to people you've never met?

Because the temptation to quit hasn't gone away. The world still pressures people to abandon their faith. Following Jesus still costs something. There are still days when the visible, comfortable, socially acceptable options look better than the invisible kingdom you can't touch yet. There are still mornings when you wake up tired and wonder if any of this is real.

Hebrews was written for those mornings.

It was written to remind you that the Jesus you trusted yesterday is the same Jesus today and will be the same Jesus forever. That his sacrifice actually worked. That his priesthood never expires. That the promises of God are backed by his own unbreakable oath. That you are part of a story that stretches from Abel to Abraham to Moses to David to you, and that the same God who sustained every one of them is sustaining you right now.

The author of Hebrews wrote to people who were thinking about giving up. His message was simple: don't. Not because the road is easy, but because the one walking it with you has already reached the end, and he's calling you home.

Ready? Let's open the letter.

Turn the page.

1

GOD'S FINAL WORD

In Homer's *The Odyssey*, a boy named Telemachus grows up without his father. Odysseus left for war before Telemachus could even remember his face. For twenty years, all the boy has are stories. Travelers bring rumors. Old soldiers share fragments. His mother Penelope tells him what she remembers. Every piece is real, every memory is true, but none of it is the same as having his father in the room.

Then one day, Odysseus comes home.

He doesn't send another messenger. He doesn't write another letter. He shows up. In person. And when Telemachus finally sees him face to face, everything changes. The fragments come together. The stories make sense. The rumors become real. Twenty years of secondhand knowledge are replaced by a living, breathing presence.

The book of Hebrews opens with a similar feel. For centuries, God had been speaking to his people. He sent prophets. He gave visions and dreams. He thundered from a mountain and whispered through a still, small voice. Every word was true. Every message was real. But it was coming in pieces, through messengers, over a very long time.

Then God did something different. He stopped sending messengers and showed up himself. Not in a cloud or a fire or a vision, but in a person. His Son. That's where Hebrews begins. And it begins with one of the most breathtaking paragraphs in the entire Bible.

GOD HAS SPOKEN

The first four verses of Hebrews pack more theology into a single paragraph than most books contain in a dozen chapters. The author doesn't waste a single word. He starts with the past, moves to the present, and lands on a statement about Jesus so enormous that the rest of the letter will spend thirteen chapters unpacking it.

"In the past God spoke to our ancestors through the prophets at many times and in various ways, but in these last days he has spoken to us by his Son." Two sentences. Two eras. Everything changes between them.

In the first sentence, God speaks through the prophets. Think about how many different ways God communicated in the Old Testament. He spoke to Moses from a burning bush. He gave the law at Sinai in thunder and lightning. He appeared to Abraham in human form. He whispered to Elijah in a quiet voice after a storm. He sent dreams to Joseph and Daniel. He gave visions to Ezekiel and Isaiah. He communicated through stories, songs, laws, proverbs, and poetry.

All of those were real revelations from God. The author of Hebrews isn't dismissing any of them. He actually loves the

Old Testament and is going to quote it more than almost any other New Testament writer. But he's pointing out something important: those revelations came in fragments. No single prophet had the whole picture. Moses saw part. David saw part. Isaiah saw part. Jeremiah heard one thing. Ezekiel saw another. Each prophet contributed a piece, like individual tiles in an enormous mosaic, but no one prophet could step back and see the finished image.

Then came the Son. And with him, the fragments came together. The mosaic was complete.

Notice what the author doesn't say. He doesn't say God sent another prophet. He doesn't say God gave another set of laws or another vision. He says God spoke "by his Son." The Son isn't just carrying a message from God the way the prophets did. He *is* the message. He is God's final, complete, nothing-left-to-say word to the human race.

SEVEN CLAIMS ABOUT THE SON

But who is this Son? The author doesn't leave us guessing. In the space of just two verses, he makes seven staggering claims about Jesus, one right after another, like a fireworks display where each explosion is bigger than the last.

First, God appointed him heir of all things. In the Old Testament, God promised the land of Canaan to Israel as their inheritance. But the Son's inheritance isn't one piece of land. It's everything. The entire created universe belongs to him. Every galaxy, every mountain, every grain of sand on every beach, every atom in every star. All of it is his.

Second, God made the universe through him. This is

where things get truly staggering. The Son didn't start existing when he was born in Bethlehem. He was there at the beginning, before the beginning, when God created everything. The baby in the manger was the same person who spoke the stars into existence.

Third, the Son is the radiance of God's glory. Imagine the sun. You can't separate the sun from its light. The light doesn't exist somewhere else, doing its own thing. It pours out from the sun and reveals what the sun is. That's what the Son does with God's glory. He shines it out. He shows the world what God looks like.

Fourth, the Son is the exact representation of God's being. In the ancient world, when a king wanted to make his authority known in a distant province, he would stamp his image on a coin. When people looked at the coin, they saw the king's face. The Son is like that, except perfectly. When you look at Jesus, you see exactly who God is. Not an approximation. Not a partial image. The real thing.

Fifth, the Son sustains all things by his powerful word. He didn't just create the universe and walk away. He holds it together right now, this second, the way a musician sustains a note. He's also driving or bearing everything to where God ultimate wants everything to be. If the Son stopped, everything would collapse. The same voice that called the world into being is the voice that keeps it running and moving to its ultimate destiny.

Sixth, the Son provided purification for sins. After everything the author has said about the Son's cosmic power and divine nature, this might seem like a sudden shift. It is. And it's the most important claim in the list. The one who created galaxies and holds atoms together also dealt with the one problem no one else could solve. He cleaned up the mess that sin had made. He did what every sacrifice in the Old Testament was pointing toward but could never fully accomplish. If you've read *What Is the Book of Exodus?* and *What Is the Book of Leviticus?*, you know how hard the Israelites worked to maintain their relationship with a holy God. The sacrifices, the rituals, the Day of Atonement. All of it was necessary, all of it was real, but none of it was permanent. The Son made it permanent.

Seventh, the Son sat down at the right hand of the Majesty in heaven. In the tabernacle and temple, the priests never sat down. There were no chairs in the holy place. Why? Because their work was never finished. There was always another sacrifice to offer, another sin to cover, another Day of Atonement to perform. But when Jesus finished his work, he sat down. The job was done. Complete. And he sat down in the place of highest honor and authority in the universe: the right hand of God himself. This single image will dominate the rest of Hebrews. The author wants his readers to see it, to fix their eyes on it, and to never look away from the Son who sits on that throne.

Seven claims. One Son. And every single one of them matters for what the author is about to say next.

GREATER THAN THE ANGELS

If you've ever seen *Ratatouille*, you know the scene where the food critic Anton Ego takes his first bite of ratatouille and is instantly transported back to his childhood. One bite, and his whole framework for understanding food changes. Everything he thought he knew about what matters in cooking gets reorganized around this one experience.

The original audience of Hebrews was going through something similar, but with much higher stakes. These were people who had grown up with a deep reverence for angels. And for good reason. In Jewish tradition, angels were the most powerful beings in the created order. They stood in God's presence. They carried out his commands. They governed nations. Most importantly, many Jewish people believed that angels had been involved in giving the law to Moses at Mount Sinai.

So when some of these early believers started wavering in their faith, it made sense that they might drift back toward a religion built on the law that angels had delivered. The angels were impressive, after all. Powerful. Otherworldly. They seemed like a safe foundation.

The author of Hebrews says: not even close.

To make his case, he does something brilliant. He lines up seven Old Testament quotations, one after another, and uses them to build an argument that the Son is not just slightly above the angels. He is in an entirely different category.

He starts with a simple question: "To which of the angels did God ever say, 'You are my Son; today I have become your Father'?" The answer is obvious. None of them. Not once. God called Israel his son. He called the kings descended from David his sons. But he never looked at an angel and said, "You are my Son." That title, that relationship, belongs to Jesus alone.

Then the author raises the stakes. When God brought his Son into the world, he commanded the angels to worship him.

Think about that. Angels don't worship each other. Angels worship God. And God told them to worship the Son. That tells you everything you need to know about who the Son is.

The contrast keeps building. The angels are servants, the author says, like wind and fire, sent to do God's bidding. They're powerful, but they're workers. The Son, on the other hand, has a throne. God the Father looks at the Son and says, "Your throne, O God, is forever and ever." God calls the Son "God." There's no way to soften that. The Son shares the identity of God himself.

And it gets even more dramatic. The author quotes a psalm originally addressed to God, the Creator, and applies it directly to the Son: "In the beginning, Lord, you laid the foundations of the earth, and the heavens are the work of your hands. They will perish, but you remain. They will all wear out like clothing. You will roll them up like a robe, and they will be changed like a garment. But you are the same, and your years will never end."

The heavens will wear out. The earth will be rolled up like an old coat. But the Son will remain unchanged forever. The angels are created beings. The Son is the Creator. They had a beginning. He had no beginning and has no end.

The author saves his best Old Testament quotation for last: "Sit at my right hand until I make your enemies a footstool for your feet." This comes from Psalm 110, the most quoted Old Testament verse in the entire New Testament, and it was the early church's favorite passage about Jesus. God never said anything like this to an angel. He never invited an angel to share his throne, to sit at his right hand as co-ruler of the universe. That invitation was for the Son alone. Angels stand in God's presence to serve. The Son sits at God's right hand to reign.

So what are the angels, then? The author answers in his final verse: "Are they not all ministering spirits sent out to serve those who will inherit salvation?" Angels are servants. The Son is sovereign. Angels serve God's people. The Son saves God's people. They work for the kingdom. He owns it.

The comparison is over. And it wasn't close.

WHAT THIS MEANS FOR US

First, God is not silent. One of the hardest things about faith is the feeling that God isn't saying anything. Maybe you've prayed and heard nothing back. Maybe you've looked for a sign and found only silence. Hebrews opens by declaring that God is a speaking God. He has been speaking for centuries, and his final, clearest word is Jesus. If you want to know what God sounds like, listen to his Son.

Second, Jesus is not just a good teacher. He's not just a prophet who came with a message from God. He is the exact representation of God's being. When you read about what Jesus said and did, you are seeing what God is like. His compassion, his honesty, his anger at injustice, his tenderness toward the broken, his willingness to suffer for people who didn't deserve it. That's God. All of it.

Third, the old and the new belong together. The author of Hebrews doesn't trash the Old Testament. He builds on it. Every quotation he uses to prove the Son's greatness comes from the scriptures that had been read and cherished for centuries. The prophets weren't wrong. They were incomplete. Jesus didn't replace the story. He completed it.

Fourth, finished means finished. The Son sat down because his work was done. In a world that constantly tells you to earn your worth, to perform your way into acceptance, to prove yourself over and over again, the gospel says something different. The sacrifice has been made. The purification is complete. You don't need to add anything to what Jesus has already accomplished.

Fifth, nothing in this universe outranks Jesus. Not angels. Not governments. Not cultural pressure. Not your worst fear. The one who created the stars and holds the universe together by his word is the same one who purified your sins and sat down at God's right hand. Whatever you're facing today is not bigger than him.

TALKING POINTS

1. **God spoke through the prophets "at many times and in various ways," but now he has spoken through his Son.** What's the difference between hearing about someone through messages and actually meeting them in person? How does this help you understand what it means that God spoke through Jesus?

2. **The author of Hebrews says the Son is "the exact representation of God's being."** When you read about Jesus in the Gospels, what specific things about him show you what God is like? Which quality of Jesus surprises you the most as a picture of God?

3. **The priests in the Old Testament never sat down because their work was never finished. But Jesus sat down at God's right hand.** What does it mean for your life that Jesus'

work is complete? How should that affect the way you think about your own relationship with God?

4. **The author goes to great lengths to show that Jesus is greater than the angels.** Why do you think it mattered so much to prove this? Are there things in your own life that seem impressive or powerful but that you might be tempted to trust more than Jesus?

5. **Hebrews 1 says the Son "sustains all things by his powerful word."** What does it mean to know that the same Jesus who loves you is also the one holding the entire universe together right now? How does that change the way you think about your problems?

The author of Hebrews has opened his letter with a paragraph so packed with truth that it will take the rest of the book to unpack it all. He's introduced us to a Son who is heir of everything, creator of the universe, the radiance of God's glory, the sustainer of all things, the purifier of sins, and the ruler seated at God's right hand. He's shown us that this Son is greater than the most powerful beings his readers could imagine.

But he hasn't told us yet what all of this means for how we live. And he hasn't told us what happens when people ignore a message this big. That's coming next, and it starts with a warning.

Turn the page.

2

THE PIONEER WHO BECAME YOUR BROTHER

In *The Call of the Wild*, a dog named Buck is stolen from a comfortable life in California and shipped to the frozen Yukon during the gold rush. He goes from sleeping by a warm fireplace to hauling sleds through blizzards. Everything he knew is stripped away. The world he enters is brutal, freezing, and deadly. But Buck doesn't just survive it. He enters it fully, becomes part of it, and eventually leads other animals through it. He becomes something he never could have been if he had stayed safe at home.

The idea of someone leaving a place of comfort and power in order to enter a harsh world and lead others through it is at the heart of Hebrews 2. But the story the author tells makes Buck's journey look like a walk in the park. Because in Hebrews 2, it's not a dog leaving California for the Yukon. It's the Son of God leaving heaven for earth. The Creator of the universe becoming a crying infant. The one who holds all things together by his powerful word choosing to experience hunger, exhaustion, pain, and death.

And he did it for a reason.

This chapter is where the letter to the Hebrews gets personal.

DON'T DRIFT AWAY

The chapter opens with a warning, and it's aimed directly at the readers. "We must pay more careful attention to what we have heard, so that we do not drift away." That word "drift" paints a picture. Imagine a boat tied to a dock. As long as the rope is secure, the boat stays put. But if the rope loosens, even slightly, the current begins to pull. The boat doesn't suddenly rocket out to sea. It drifts. Slowly. Quietly. The person sitting in it might not even notice until the shore is far behind them.

That's what the author is worried about. He isn't writing to people who have openly rejected Jesus. He's writing to people who are slowly, quietly, almost imperceptibly letting go. They're tired. Life is hard. The excitement of their early faith has faded. And instead of holding on more tightly, they're loosening their grip.

His argument is simple and devastating. If the message delivered through angels at Mount Sinai was binding, and every violation of it brought consequences, then what happens to people who ignore a message delivered by God's own Son? "How shall we escape if we neglect such a great salvation?"

Notice the word "neglect." The author isn't talking about attacking the gospel or mocking it. He's talking about ignoring it. Treating it as unimportant. Moving on to other things. The danger he sees isn't rebellion. It's indifference. And indifference toward a message this big, delivered by a messenger this great, is not something anyone can afford.

The salvation he's describing isn't small. It was first spoken by the Lord himself. It was confirmed by eyewitnesses. God backed it up with signs, wonders, miracles, and gifts of the Holy Spirit. Every possible form of confirmation has been given. The evidence is overwhelming. The only question is whether the readers will pay attention.

BUT WE DO SEE JESUS

Then the author does something unexpected. After spending all of chapter 1 proving that the Son is greater than the angels, he now turns around and talks about how the Son became *lower* than them.

He starts with a question about the future. "It is not to angels that God has subjected the world to come." Whatever God has planned for the future of his creation, angels aren't in charge of it. So who is?

To answer, the author reaches back to Psalm 8. That psalm is a song of wonder about humanity. The psalmist looks up at the night sky and asks, "What is man that you are mindful of him, the son of man that you care for him?" Compared to the vastness of the stars, human beings seem impossibly small. And yet God gave them an astonishing destiny: "You made him a little lower than the angels. You crowned him with glory and honor and put everything under his feet."

That was the plan from the beginning. Back in Genesis, God created human beings to rule over the earth, to be his representatives, his stewards over creation. Humanity was made for glory and dominion.

But here's the problem: "We do not yet see everything subject to him." Look around. Does it look like human beings are ruling the world the way God intended? It doesn't. Sin has wrecked everything. Instead of reigning over creation, humanity is enslaved to fear, death, and brokenness. The glorious destiny described in Psalm 8 feels like a dream that never came true.

And then comes one of the most important sentences in the entire letter: "But we do see Jesus." We don't see humanity fulfilling its destiny. But we do see one human who did. Jesus was made lower than the angels. He took on human flesh. He entered our world with all its suffering and limitations. And then, because of his suffering and death, he was crowned with glory and honor. He did what the rest of us couldn't do. He lived the human life we were supposed to live, died the death we deserved to die, and was exalted to the place of honor we were always meant to have.

And here's the stunning part: he didn't do it for himself. He tasted death "for everyone." That phrase means he experienced death in its fullness, with all its bitterness and horror, not for his own sake but for ours. His suffering wasn't an accident. It was the plan. "By the grace of God," the author says, Jesus tasted death so that we wouldn't have to face it alone.

THE PIONEER OF OUR SALVATION

The next verse might be the most shocking statement in the chapter. "It was fitting that God, for whom and through whom everything exists, in bringing many sons and daughters to glory, should make the pioneer of their salvation perfect through suffering." Read that again. God made the pioneer of our salvation perfect *through suffering*.

The word "pioneer" is rich. A pioneer is someone who goes first into unknown, dangerous territory so that others can follow. Think Daniel Boone and Davy Crockett. Think of the trailblazers who crossed unmapped wilderness so that settlers could come after them. Jesus is the pioneer of our salvation. He blazed the trail through suffering, through death, through the grave, and out the other side into glory. And now he's leading his people down that same path.

But what does it mean that God made him "perfect through suffering"? It doesn't mean Jesus was flawed and needed improvement. It means that through his suffering, he was fully equipped and qualified for his role as Savior. A doctor who has never been sick can still treat patients. But a doctor who has suffered the same illness you have understands your experience from the inside. Jesus didn't just observe human suffering from heaven. He entered it. He felt it. And because he went through it, he is perfectly qualified to lead others through it.

Then the author says something that would have made his original readers' jaws drop: "Both the one who makes people holy and those who are being made holy are of the same family. So Jesus is not ashamed to call them brothers and sisters."

Think about what chapter 1 just told us. The Son is the radiance of God's glory. He created the universe. He sustains all things by his powerful word. God the Father calls him "God." And this same Son looks at struggling, stumbling, failing human believers and says, "Those are my brothers and sisters. And I'm proud of it."

He's not embarrassed by us. He's not keeping his distance. He chose to join the family. And to prove it, the author quotes three Old Testament passages where the Son speaks. In the first, from Psalm 22, the Son says, "I will declare your name to my brothers and sisters. In the midst of the congregation I will sing your praises." That psalm begins with the cry Jesus shouted from the cross: "My God, my God, why have you forsaken me?" It ends with praise and triumph. The suffering Son became the singing Son, and he sings in the company of the people he saved.

In the second and third quotations, from Isaiah, the Son declares his trust in God and then says, "Here am I, and the children God has given me." Jesus doesn't just tolerate us. He presents us to the Father with joy, the way a big brother might introduce his younger siblings to a room full of strangers: "These are mine. They belong with me."

WHY HE HAD TO BECOME LIKE US

Now the author explains why the Son had to become human. The reason goes deeper than most people expect. "Since the children have flesh and blood, he too shared in their humanity so that by his death he might destroy him who holds the power of death, that is, the devil, and free those who all their lives were held in slavery by their fear of death."

This is one of the most dramatic statements in the New Testament. Human beings were trapped. Death hung over every moment of their lives like a shadow they could never escape. And behind that shadow stood the devil, using death as a weapon to keep people in chains. Not physical chains, but something worse: the fear that death is the final word, that everything ends in the grave, that nothing we do ultimately matters.

The Son entered that prison. He took on flesh and blood. He became as vulnerable as the people he came to save. And then he did the one thing no one expected: he died. The Author of life submitted to death. But in dying, he destroyed the power of the one who wielded death. He broke the weapon by letting it strike him. He defeated death by going through it and coming out the other side alive.

This is why the incarnation (Jesus becoming flesh and blood) matters so much. The Son didn't help from a distance. He didn't send instructions from heaven. He came down, put on skin, and entered the fight personally. The author makes this explicit: "It is not angels he helps, but Abraham's descendants." The Son didn't become an angel. He became a human being, because human beings were the ones who needed rescuing.

A MERCIFUL AND FAITHFUL HIGH PRIEST

The chapter ends with two verses that introduce the most important concept in the entire letter: "For this reason he had to be made like his brothers and sisters in every way, in order that he might become a merciful and faithful high priest in service to God, and that he might make atonement for the sins of the people. Because he himself suffered when he was tempted, he is able to help those who are being tempted." There it is. The phrase the whole letter has been building toward: *high priest.*

The high priest was the one person who could enter God's presence on behalf of the people. He carried their sins to the altar. He stood between a holy God and an unholy people and made it possible for them to be in relationship.

Jesus is that high priest. But he's better than Aaron ever was, because he didn't just represent the people from the outside. He became one of them. He was "made like his brothers and sisters in every way." He knows what it feels like to be tired, hungry, lonely, tempted, misunderstood, and afraid. He knows what it feels like to suffer. And because he knows all of that from personal experience, he is able to be *merciful.* He doesn't look at struggling people and say, "What's wrong with you?" He looks at them and says, "I know. I've been there. And I can help."

That last verse is one of the most comforting sentences in the Bible. "Because he himself suffered when he was tempted, he is able to help those who are being tempted." He's not a distant God watching from the sky. He's a Savior who walked the road before you, who felt every pothole and sharp stone, and who stands at the other end reaching back to pull you through.

WHAT THIS MEANS FOR US

First, drifting is more dangerous than rebellion. Most people don't walk away from faith in one dramatic moment. They drift. Slowly, quietly, a little bit at a time, until one day they look up and realize they're far from where they started. The author of Hebrews warns us to pay attention. Hold the rope. Don't let the current carry you away without a fight.

Second, your destiny is bigger than you think. Psalm 8 says human beings were made for glory and honor. Sin has distorted that picture, but it hasn't erased it. In Jesus, the original plan is being restored. If you belong to him, you are headed for a glory you can barely imagine. Your small, ordinary life is part of a story that ends with you sharing in the reign of the Son of God.

Third, Jesus chose to become like you. He didn't have to. No one forced the Son of God to put on flesh and blood. He chose it. He chose hunger, exhaustion, temptation, pain, and death because he loved the people he came to save. When you feel like nobody understands what you're going through, remember that the Son of God became a human being specifically so he could understand.

Fourth, the fear of death has been broken. You may not feel free from it yet. The shadow may still seem real. But the author of Hebrews says that Jesus entered death, destroyed its power, and set free everyone who was enslaved by its fear. Death is not the final word. The pioneer has already gone through it, and he's calling you to follow him into glory.

Fifth, your high priest is not distant. He is merciful because he has suffered. He is faithful because he has been tested. He doesn't help you from across the universe. He helps you as someone who has been exactly where you are. Whatever you're facing today, he is able to help.

TALKING POINTS

1. **The author warns about "drifting away" from the faith.** What does spiritual drifting look like in everyday life? What are the small things that can slowly pull someone away from paying attention to God?

2. **Psalm 8 says God made human beings "a little lower than the angels" and crowned them with "glory and honor."** What does it mean that our destiny as human beings is tied to Jesus? How does his victory change what the future looks like for you?

3. **Jesus is called "the pioneer of salvation."** What does a pioneer do? How does knowing that Jesus walked the path of suffering before you change the way you face your own hard times?

4. **The author says Jesus is "not ashamed" to call Christians his brothers and sisters.** Why is that such a big deal, given everything chapter 1 told us about who the Son is? What does it feel like to know that the Creator of the universe calls you family?

5. **Hebrews 2:18 says Jesus "is able to help those who are being tempted" because he himself was tempted and suffered.** How is this different from someone who gives you advice about something they've never experienced? How does it change the way you pray, knowing your high priest has been where you are?

The author of Hebrews has done something remarkable in this chapter. He took the exalted Son from chapter 1, the one who created the universe and outranks every angel, and showed us that same Son entering our world, sharing our flesh, suffering our pain, and dying our death. Not because he had to. Because he wanted to. Because that was the only way to become the kind of Savior we actually needed: one who is both powerful enough to save us and close enough to understand us.

He is our pioneer. He is our brother. And he is our high priest.

That last title is going to change everything. The author has only just introduced it, but he's going to spend the rest of this letter explaining what it means. And what it means will reshape how we think about God, about worship, about forgiveness, and about how we live every single day.

Turn the page.

3

DON'T STOP NOW

Have you ever read Robert Louis Stevenson's *Treasure Island*? In the book, the voyage begins with everything a young adventurer could hope for. Jim Hawkins has a treasure map. He has a ship. He has a crew of strong sailors and a respected captain. He has a clear destination: an island full of buried gold. Everything is pointing in the right direction.

But by the middle of the story, things have gone horribly wrong. Most of the crew turns out to be pirates. A mutiny erupts. The very men who were supposed to help Jim reach the treasure are now trying to kill him. The voyage that started with such promise nearly ends in disaster, not because the treasure wasn't real, but because the people on the ship stopped trusting the captain and went their own way.

Hebrews 3–4 tell a story like that, except it's not fiction. It's the true account of a nation that had the most incredible beginning in human history and still managed to miss everything God had promised them. They walked out of slavery in Egypt. They crossed the Red Sea on dry ground. They ate bread that fell from heaven every morning. They had the visible presence of God leading them as a pillar of cloud by day and fire by night. And when they reached the border of the land God had promised them, they refused to go in.

The author of Hebrews reaches back into this story because he sees his readers heading down the same path. They started well. But they're slowing down. They're looking back. And if they don't pay attention, they could lose everything.

GREATER THAN MOSES

Before getting to the wilderness disaster, the author sets up a comparison that would have been explosive for his original audience. He puts Jesus next to Moses.

You know who Moses was. He was the most revered figure in all of Israel's history. He confronted Pharaoh. He led the people out of Egypt. He parted the Red Sea. He received the Ten Commandments directly from God on Mount Sinai. He set up the entire sacrificial system, the priesthood, and the tabernacle. Everything in Israel's worship traced back to Moses. To a Jewish person, saying someone was greater than Moses was like saying someone was greater than the founding fathers, the greatest general, and the most beloved teacher all rolled into one.

The author of Hebrews says it anyway.

He starts with what Moses and Jesus have in common: both were faithful. God entrusted Moses with an enormous responsibility, and Moses carried it out. He was faithful "in all God's house," which means the entire community of God's people. The author doesn't minimize that. He honors Moses' faithfulness.

But then he draws a distinction that changes everything. Moses was faithful *in* God's house. Jesus is faithful *over* God's house. Moses was a servant inside the household. Jesus is the Son who built it.

Think of it this way. A house manager might be incredibly skilled, trustworthy, and dedicated. But the manager is not the architect. The manager works inside the house. The architect designed and built it. The honor due the builder is always greater than the honor due the building or anyone who works inside it.

Moses served as a faithful steward in God's household. He pointed forward to something greater that was coming. The entire system he established, the sacrifices, the priesthood, the tabernacle, all of it was a signpost pointing toward a future reality. Moses was a witness to what would be spoken in the future. He was the greatest preview in the Old Testament of what God would eventually do through his Son.

But the Son isn't a preview. He's the main event.

Then comes the line that ties this directly to the readers: "And we are his house, if we hold on to our courage and the hope of which we boast." The author includes himself. We are God's house. We are the people over whom the Son presides. But that identity comes with a condition: hold on. Don't let go of your confidence. Don't let go of the hope that brought you to faith in the first place.

That word "if" is not meant to create doubt. It's meant to create urgency.

THE REBELLION AT KADESH

With that urgency in place, the author reaches for Psalm 95, a passage every Jewish person would have recognized immediately. It was used as a call to worship every Sabbath in the synagogue. The opening words were deeply familiar: "Today, if you hear his voice, do not harden your hearts."

But the psalm doesn't stop with a general call to listen. It points to a specific disaster. It reaches back to the story of the wilderness generation, the people Moses led out of Egypt, and it tells what happened when they stopped listening.

Here's the short version of that story, from the book of Numbers. After all the miracles in Egypt, after the Red Sea, after the manna and the water from the rock, God brought his people to the edge of the Promised Land at a place called Kadesh-Barnea. Moses sent twelve spies into the land to scout it out. Ten came back terrified. "The people there are giants," they said. "The cities are fortified. We can't take that land. We looked like grasshoppers compared to them."

Only two spies, Joshua and Caleb, trusted God. "We should go in," they said. "God promised us this land. He can handle the giants."

The people sided with the ten. They panicked. They wept. They talked about going back to Egypt. They even talked about stoning Joshua and Caleb for daring to suggest they trust God.

And God responded with devastating judgment. The entire generation, everyone twenty years old and older except Joshua and Caleb, would die in the wilderness. They would wander for forty years until the last rebel was buried in the sand. The land God had promised them, the land flowing with milk and honey, would be given to their children instead.

That's the story the author of Hebrews puts in front of his readers. And he makes it personal.

THE DANGER OF UNBELIEF

"See to it, brothers and sisters, that none of you has a sinful, unbelieving heart that turns away from the living God." The word "unbelief" is the author's diagnosis of everything that went wrong in the wilderness. The people didn't fail because the giants were too big. They failed because they didn't believe God was bigger. They had seen the plagues. They had walked through the sea. They had eaten bread from heaven every single morning. And when God said, "Go into the land I'm giving you," they said, "No. We can't. It's too hard."

That's what unbelief looks like. It doesn't always announce itself as rejection of God. Sometimes it looks like exhaustion. Sometimes it looks like fear. Sometimes it looks like a slow, quiet decision that the obstacles in front of you are more real than the promises behind you.

The author isn't describing people who never believed. He's describing people who started believing and then stopped. That's what makes it so frightening. The wilderness generation wasn't a group of atheists. They were God's people. They had experienced his power firsthand. And they still turned away.

So the author gives his readers a prescription: "Encourage one another daily, as long as it is called 'today,' so that none of you may be hardened by sin's deceitfulness." The antidote to drifting is community. You fight unbelief not by gritting your teeth harder in isolation but by surrounding yourself with people who remind you of what's true. The word "encourage" here means more than just being nice. It means speaking truth into each other's lives, warning each other when you see someone starting to slip, and refusing to let anyone drift away alone.

If the movie *Finding Dory* teaches us anything, it's that the journey is harder when you try to do it by yourself. Dory keeps getting lost and forgetting where she's going. But every time she's surrounded by friends who remind her of her purpose, she finds her way again. The author of Hebrews is telling his readers the same thing. You need each other. Every single day. Because sin is deceitful, and it will convince you to give up if you let it.

The chapter closes with a grim summary. Who rebelled? Everyone who came out of Egypt. Who made God angry for forty years? Those who sinned. Whose bodies fell in the desert? The disobedient. Who was shut out of God's rest? Those who refused to believe. The pattern is relentless: unbelief leads to disobedience, disobedience leads to judgment, and judgment means missing what God had planned for you.

A REST THAT STILL REMAINS

But here's where the author does something unexpected. Instead of ending with the tragedy, he pivots. If the wilderness generation lost God's "rest" through unbelief, then that rest must still be available for someone else.

"Therefore, since the promise of entering his rest still stands, let us be careful that none of you be found to have fallen short of it." The rest isn't gone. It's still there. The wilderness generation refused it, but God didn't cancel it. He promised his people a destination, and that promise outlasted every person who rejected it.

But what exactly is this "rest"? The author spends several verses working through the answer. He starts with creation. When God finished making the world, he rested on the seventh day. Not because he was tired, but because the work was complete. That rest, God's own rest, has existed since the foundation of the world.

Then he points out that Joshua eventually led the next generation into the Promised Land of Canaan. But even that wasn't the real rest. How do we know? Because hundreds of years later, in Psalm 95, God was still offering his rest to his people. "Today, if you hear his voice." If the Promised Land had been the ultimate rest, God wouldn't still be inviting people into something more.

The rest God is talking about is bigger than a piece of land. It's God's own rest. His eternal dwelling. The place where struggle ends and celebration begins. The author calls it a "Sabbath rest," a word that brings to mind not just cessation of work but joyful worship, the kind of rest that feels like a feast rather than a nap. It's the heavenly homeland that the faithful have been longing for since Abraham first packed up and followed God's call.

And it's still available. "There remains, then, a Sabbath rest for the people of God." That sentence is meant to fill the readers with hope and urgency at the same time. Hope, because the promise hasn't expired. God's rest is real, and it's waiting. Urgency, because the wilderness generation proves that it's possible to come right up to the edge and still miss it. "Let us, therefore, make every effort to enter that rest, so that no one will fall by following their example of disobedience."

THE LIVING WORD OF GOD

Then the author drops one of the most famous passages in the entire Bible. It comes almost out of nowhere, like a thunder-clap after a long, building storm.

"For the word of God is living and active. Sharper than any double-edged sword, it penetrates even to dividing soul and spirit, joints and marrow; it judges the thoughts and attitudes of the heart. Nothing in all creation is hidden from God's sight. Everything is uncovered and laid bare before the eyes of him to whom we must give account."

This is the author's way of saying: you cannot hide from what God has spoken. His word isn't a dusty book sitting on a shelf. It's alive. It moves. It cuts through every layer of self-deception and pretense and gets to the truth of who you really are and what you really believe.

The wilderness generation thought they could ignore God's promises and face no consequences. They were wrong. The readers of Hebrews might be tempted to think they can slowly drift away and no one will notice. The author says: God notices. His word sees everything. Every thought, every motive, every hidden corner of the heart is exposed before him.

This isn't meant to terrify. It's meant to wake people up. You are accountable to a God who sees everything, who keeps his promises, and who has offered you something so magnificent that ignoring it would be the greatest tragedy of your life.

WHAT THIS MEANS FOR US

First, a great start doesn't guarantee a great finish. The wilderness generation had the most spectacular beginning imaginable. Miracles, deliverance, God's visible presence. And they still fell short. Your spiritual history matters, but it doesn't protect you if you stop trusting God today. Faith is not a one-time event. It's a daily decision.

Second, Jesus is greater than every spiritual hero. Moses was extraordinary. But he was a servant in the house. Jesus is the Son over the house. Whatever human leader, teacher, or tradition you admire most, Jesus stands above them all. He isn't just part of the story. He's the one the whole story is about.

Third, you need other people. The command to "encourage one another daily" is not optional. Spiritual life was never meant to be lived alone. You need people who will remind you of the truth when you're tempted to forget it. And someone around you needs you to do the same for them.

Fourth, God's rest is still waiting for you. The promise hasn't expired. Whatever God has planned for his people, it's still ahead. The failures of the past don't cancel God's future. But you have to keep walking toward it. You have to keep trusting.

Fifth, God's word sees the real you. You can fool other people. You can even fool yourself. But you can't fool the word of God. It knows your thoughts, your motives, your fears, and your doubts. And that's actually good news, because a God who sees everything is also a God who can heal everything.

TALKING POINTS

1. **The wilderness generation had seen incredible miracles but still refused to trust God at Kadesh-Barnea.** Why do you think experiencing God's power doesn't automatically

produce lasting faith? What does it take for faith to survive when things get hard?

2. **The author says we are God's house "if we hold on to our courage and the hope of which we boast."** What does it look like to hold on to spiritual courage in your everyday life? What makes people let go?

3. **"Encourage one another daily" is the author's prescription for avoiding a hardened heart.** What does real encouragement look like, not just being nice, but speaking truth to each other? Who in your life encourages you this way, and who might need you to do this for them?

4. **God's "rest" is described as something bigger than the Promised Land, something that's been waiting since the creation of the world.** What do you think this rest will be like? How does looking forward to it change the way you handle hard things now?

5. **The word of God is described as "living and active" and able to judge "the thoughts and attitudes of the heart."** How is this different from the way most people think about the Bible? What does it feel like to know that God sees not just your actions but your deepest thoughts and motives?

The wilderness generation's story is over. Their bodies are buried in the sand. The rest they were offered, they never received. But the promise remains. It's still open. It's still real. And the author of Hebrews has been building toward something that will make all the difference for his readers: the high priest who can actually get them there. He's been hinting at it since chapter 2. Now he's about to explain what it means.

Turn the page.

4

A PRIEST WHO UNDERSTANDS

In Charles Dickens' *A Christmas Carol*, Ebenezer Scrooge is a man of enormous power and zero compassion. He has wealth. He has influence. But when his clerk Bob Cratchit asks for a day off on Christmas, Scrooge can barely contain his contempt. When he's asked to donate to charity, he suggests the poor should die and "decrease the surplus population." He doesn't understand suffering because he has walled himself off from it. He lives in a different world from the people around him, and he has no interest in crossing over.

Then the ghosts come. They don't just show Scrooge other people's pain from a distance. They drag him into it. He stands in the Cratchit home and watches Tiny Tim, the crippled boy who may not survive the year. He sees his own past loneliness. He feels the cold grip of death itself. And when it's over, Scrooge is a completely different man. Not because he learned new information, but because he *experienced* what others had experienced. Sympathy changed everything.

Hebrews 4:14–5:10 introduces us to a High Priest who didn't just observe human suffering from a distance. He entered it. He felt every bit of it. And because he did, he became the kind of Savior who doesn't look down at struggling people and say, "Try harder." He looks at them and says, "I know. Come to me. I have exactly what you need."

A GREAT HIGH PRIEST

The author of Hebrews has been building toward this moment since chapter 2, when he first called Jesus a "merciful and faithful high priest." He mentioned it again in chapter 3, when he told his readers to "fix your thoughts on Jesus, the apostle and high priest whom we confess." Now, finally, he stops hinting and starts explaining.

"Since we have a great high priest who has passed through the heavens, Jesus the Son of God, let us hold firmly to the faith we profess." Every word here matters. This high priest is "great," a word that in the original language is almost redundant. A high priest is already the highest priest. Calling him "great" on top of that is like saying the highest of the high, the greatest of the great. This isn't just any priest.

He "has passed through the heavens." If you remember the tabernacle from Exodus and Leviticus, you know that the high priest entered the Most Holy Place once a year on the Day of Atonement. He walked through the outer courtyard, through the Holy Place, through the thick curtain, and into the inner room where God's presence dwelt above the ark of the covenant. It was the most sacred journey in Israel's worship. But it was temporary. The high priest went in, sprinkled the blood, and came right back out.

Jesus didn't pass through a curtain into an earthly tent. He passed through the heavens themselves and sat down at the right hand of God. He entered the real presence of God, the ultimate Holy of Holies, and he's still there. The access he opened isn't temporary. It's permanent. The door he walked through stays open.

And he is both "Jesus" and "the Son of God." Those two titles held together are the foundation of everything. He is Jesus, the fully human one who walked on dusty roads and got tired and hungry and sad. And he is the Son of God, the eternal one through whom the universe was made. Both are true at the same time. Both matter for what comes next.

Because of who this High Priest is, the author says, we should hold firmly to our confession. Don't let go. Don't drift. Don't waver. You have a High Priest powerful enough to sustain you through anything.

A PRIEST WHO SYMPATHIZES

But power alone isn't enough. You can admire someone powerful and still feel like they don't understand you. A king on a distant throne might have the authority to help, but if he's never left the palace, you might wonder whether he knows what your life is actually like.

So the author adds something that changes everything. "For we do not have a high priest who is unable to sympathize with our weaknesses, but we have one who has been tempted in every way, just as we are, yet was without sin." Read that again. This is one of the most comforting verses in the entire Bible.

The old high priest in Israel could be gentle with struggling people because he was a sinner himself. He knew what it felt like to fail. That gave him some compassion, but it also made him weak. He had to offer a sacrifice for his own sins before he could do anything for the people. His gentleness came from shared failure.

Jesus' compassion comes from something different. He was tempted in every way we are, but he never sinned. He knows what temptation feels like, not from the outside, but from the inside. He felt its full force. In fact, he experienced temptation more intensely than any human being ever has, precisely *because* he never gave in. Think of it this way: if you're standing in a hurricane and you let the wind knock you down after five seconds, you've only felt five seconds of the storm's power. But if you stand against it for the full duration, fighting every gust, you experience the storm's complete fury. Jesus never gave in. He stood against every temptation for an entire lifetime, all the way to the cross. No one has ever been tested like he was.

And because of that, he doesn't just feel sorry for us. He sympathizes. That word means more than pity. It means he shares in the experience. When you're struggling with something, your High Priest doesn't look at you from across the universe and offer generic advice. He feels it with you because he has been where you are.

This leads to one of the most beautiful invitations in all of Scripture: "Let us then approach the throne of grace with confidence, so that we may receive mercy and find grace to help us in our time of need."

Under the old system, the throne of God was a terrifying place. It was the seat of judgment. The ark of the covenant in the Most Holy Place was called the "mercy seat," but approaching it without the right preparation could kill you.

Only one person, one day a year, with the blood of a sacrifice, could go near it.

Now that throne is called a throne of grace. Not because God has become less holy, but because Jesus' sacrifice has dealt with the sin that made it dangerous. The barrier is gone. The door is open. And God's people are invited, not to tiptoe in with fear, but to come with confidence. The word "confidence" doesn't mean arrogance. It means the freedom to speak openly, the way you would talk to someone who loves you and has already told you you're welcome.

And what do you find when you come? Mercy for your past and grace for your future. Mercy covers what you've done wrong. Grace gives you the strength to keep going. Both are available right now, at exactly the moment you need them.

HOW JESUS QUALIFIES

Having told his readers what kind of High Priest they have, the author now explains how Jesus qualifies for the job. He does this by comparing Jesus with the priests descended from Aaron.

An Old Testament high priest had to meet certain qualifications. First, he was taken from among human beings. He wasn't an angel or a supernatural being. He was a man, chosen from the people he would represent. Second, he was appointed to act on behalf of people "in things pertaining to God," which mainly meant offering sacrifices for sin. Third, he could deal gently with sinners because he was a sinner himself. He knew what weakness felt like because he was wrapped in it. Fourth, he didn't choose himself for the job. God chose him. Aaron didn't volunteer. God called him.

Jesus meets every one of these qualifications, but in each case he surpasses the original.

Was Jesus taken from among human beings? Yes. He became fully human. He didn't pretend to be human or borrow a human body for a while. He lived an entire human life, from infancy to death.

Was he appointed by God? Absolutely. The author quotes two Old Testament passages to prove it. First, Psalm 2: "You are my Son; today I have become your Father." Then Psalm 110: "You are a priest forever, in the order of Melchizedek." God himself declared Jesus both Son and Priest. He didn't take the honor on himself. The Father gave it to him.

That name "Melchizedek" shows up here for the first time, and the author is going to spend a lot of time on it later. For now, what matters is this: Melchizedek was a mysterious figure from Genesis 14 who was both a king and a priest. Aaron's priesthood was inherited and temporary. Every Aaronic priest eventually died and was replaced. But Psalm 110 declares a priesthood that is "forever," one that belongs to a completely different order. Jesus is that priest. His priesthood doesn't expire.

Could Jesus deal gently with struggling people? This is where the author reaches the emotional peak of the passage. "During the days of Jesus' life on earth, he offered up prayers and petitions with loud cries and tears to the one who could save him from death, and he was heard because of his reverent submission."

Loud cries. Tears. This isn't the serene, untouchable Jesus of stained-glass windows. This is a man in agony. Most readers think of Gethsemane, the night before the cross, when Jesus fell on the ground and begged his Father to take the cup of suffering away from him. His sweat fell like drops of blood. He was in such anguish that an angel came to strengthen him. And he prayed not once but three times.

But the author of Hebrews isn't limiting this to one night. He says "during the days of his life on earth," suggesting that this kind of desperate, dependent prayer characterized Jesus' entire human experience. He lived as someone who needed God every single day. He didn't coast through life on divine autopilot. He prayed. He wept. He cried out. And God heard him.

Then comes a verse that sounds strange at first: "Although he was a son, he learned obedience from what he suffered." This doesn't mean Jesus was disobedient and then got better. It means he experienced what obedience costs. Obedience is easy when nothing is at stake. But obedience when the world is pushing back, when doing the right thing brings pain and rejection and death, that kind of obedience has to be lived through. Jesus learned it not by failing and trying again, but by succeeding under pressure that would have crushed anyone else. Each act of faithfulness in the face of suffering deepened his experience of what it means to trust God completely.

The old high priest was "beset with weakness." His life was defined by his own limitations and failures. Jesus' life was defined by obedience. That's the contrast. One priest was shaped by sin. The other was shaped by faithfulness.

And the result? "Once made perfect, he became the source of eternal salvation for all who obey him, and was designated by God to be high priest in the order of Melchizedek."

"Made perfect" means he was fully qualified, completely equipped for his role as Savior. Not that he was flawed before, but that through his suffering and obedience he became everything a High Priest needs to be. He is now the "source" of salvation. Not a temporary fix. Not an annual ritual that has to be repeated. An eternal, never-ending, always-available source of rescue for everyone who trusts him.

WHAT THIS MEANS FOR US

First, you can come to God right now. The throne room is open. The High Priest has gone ahead of you and made the way safe. You don't need to clean yourself up first. You don't need to earn the right to pray. You come as you are, and you find mercy and grace waiting for you. That invitation isn't for perfect people. It's for desperate ones.

Second, Jesus understands what you're going through. He's not a distant God who watches your struggles from far away. He lived them. He felt temptation, loneliness, grief, exhaustion, and fear. When you tell him what you're going through, he doesn't just hear the words. He knows the feeling. His sympathy isn't theoretical. It's earned.

Third, weakness and sin are not the same thing. The old high priest was beset with weakness *and* sin. Jesus experienced weakness, hunger, exhaustion, grief, and the full weight of human limitation, but never sin. That means your own struggles and weaknesses don't disqualify you from coming to God. You don't have to be strong to approach the throne of grace. You just have to come.

Fourth, obedience gets harder before it gets easier. Jesus "learned obedience through what he suffered." Following God doesn't always feel good. Sometimes it costs everything. But the path Jesus walked, the path of faithful obedience even when it hurts, is the same path that leads to glory. If the Son of God learned obedience through suffering, we shouldn't be surprised when our own obedience is tested by hard things.

Fifth, this High Priest is forever. Aaron's priests died. They were replaced. The sacrifices they offered had to be repeated year after year. But Jesus is a priest "forever, in the order of Melchizedek." His work doesn't expire. His intercession doesn't stop. His sympathy doesn't run out. Whatever you need from him today, he will still be the source of it tomorrow, and the day after that, and for all eternity.

TALKING POINTS

1. **The author calls God's throne a "throne of grace" and invites us to approach it "with confidence."** What makes it hard for people to come to God honestly? What would change in your prayer life if you truly believed you were welcome?

2. **Jesus was "tempted in every way, just as we are, yet was without sin."** Why does it matter that he was tempted but never sinned? How is his sympathy different from the sympathy of someone who has failed in the same way you have?

3. **The old high priest had to offer a sacrifice for his own sins before he could help anyone else. Jesus didn't.** What does that tell you about the difference between the help they could offer and the help Jesus offers?

4. **Hebrews says Jesus "offered up prayers and petitions with loud cries and tears."** How does knowing that Jesus

prayed this way change the way you think about your own prayers? Is it okay to be desperate when you pray?

5. **Jesus "learned obedience from what he suffered."** What does it look like for you to practice obedience when it's hard? Can you think of a time when doing the right thing cost you something? How did that experience shape you?

The author of Hebrews has done what he set out to do. He's shown his readers the kind of High Priest they have: one who is both the Son of God and a tested, suffering, sympathetic human being. One who passed through the heavens and sat down at God's right hand. One who turned the throne of judgment into a throne of grace. One who is the source, not of temporary relief, but of eternal salvation.

But the author isn't done. He has more to say about this mysterious priesthood "in the order of Melchizedek." And before he gets there, he has something difficult to tell his readers. Something they might not want to hear.

Turn the page.

5

GROW UP OR FALL AWAY

Have you ever watched someone with incredible talent just quit? Maybe it was a kid on your team who was faster, stronger, or more skilled than everyone else but stopped showing up to practice.

In *Great Expectations*, Charles Dickens gives us Miss Havisham, a woman who stopped growing the day she was jilted at the altar. She never took off her wedding dress. She never cleared the rotting wedding cake from the table. She let the clocks stop. She chose to stay frozen in the worst moment of her life rather than move forward. And the longer she stayed still, the more twisted and bitter she became. Dickens is showing us something the author of Hebrews understood perfectly: when you stop growing, you don't just stay where you are. You decay.

That's the warning at the heart of Hebrews 5:11–6:12. The author has just introduced the most important concept in his entire letter, the high priesthood of Jesus "in the order of Melchizedek." He has more to say about it, much more, and it's the kind of teaching that could change his readers' lives forever. But he stops. He pauses mid-thought and says something his readers probably didn't want to hear.

"You're not ready for this."

MILK AND SOLID FOOD

The author's frustration is hard to miss. "We have much to say about this, but it is hard to explain because you are slow to learn." He doesn't say the material is too complicated. He says the problem is with his audience. They've become "dull of hearing," a phrase that literally suggests ears that have gone sluggish. Not because they can't understand, but because they've stopped trying. They've become spiritually lazy.

Then he twists the knife a little deeper. "By this time you ought to be teachers, yet you need someone to teach you the elementary truths of God's word all over again. You need milk, not solid food!" Think about what he's saying. These are people who have been Christians long enough that they should be helping others learn the faith. Instead, they need to be retaught the basics. It's as if a high school student suddenly needed to go back and relearn the alphabet. Not because they never knew it, but because they let it slip away through neglect.

The image of milk and solid food is deliberately humiliating. In the ancient world, just as today, milk was for infants. There's nothing wrong with a baby drinking milk. But there's something deeply wrong with a grown adult who can't handle anything else. The author is painting a picture designed to make his readers' faces burn with shame: you are spiritual babies when you should be spiritual adults.

He draws the contrast sharply. "Anyone who lives on milk

is still an infant, not acquainted with the teaching about righteousness. But solid food is for the mature, who by constant use have trained themselves to distinguish good from evil."

The mature aren't people who happened to stumble into wisdom. They're people who trained. They practiced. They exercised their spiritual senses the way an athlete exercises muscles, day after day, until they developed the ability to discern what's true and what's false, what's right and what's dangerous. The word picture here is athletic. Just as a runner builds endurance through daily training, a mature Christian builds spiritual discernment through constant engagement with God's word and constant practice of faithfulness. You don't develop the ability to tell good from evil by sitting on the sideline. You develop it by getting in the game and staying there.

Maturity doesn't happen by accident. It's the result of showing up, paying attention, and doing the hard work of growing. And the "solid food" that produces it isn't some secret, advanced knowledge available only to spiritual experts. It's the deep truth about who Jesus is, what his sacrifice accomplished, and how his ongoing priesthood sustains his people. That's what the author wants to teach them. That's what they need. And that's what their spiritual laziness is preventing them from receiving.

The author's point is clear: there is no such thing as standing still in the spiritual life. You're either moving forward toward maturity or sliding backward toward the kind of dullness that puts you in danger. And his readers are sliding.

MOVE ON TO MATURITY

So what does he do? He doesn't go back and re-teach the basics. He pushes forward. "Therefore, let us move beyond the elementary teachings about Christ and be taken forward to maturity."

He lists six foundational teachings that every believer should already know: repentance from dead works, faith in God, instruction about baptisms, the laying on of hands, the resurrection of the dead, and eternal judgment. These aren't unimportant. They're essential. But they're the foundation, not the building. You don't keep re-pouring a foundation over and over. You build on it.

The solid food the author wants to serve his readers is the teaching about Christ's high priesthood, the truth that will sustain them through suffering and keep them from falling away. It's the spiritual nourishment they desperately need. And he's about to give it to them, but first he has to wake them up to the danger of staying where they are.

Because staying where they are could lead somewhere terrible.

A WARNING THAT CANNOT BE IGNORED

What comes next is one of the most debated and most alarming passages in the entire New Testament. "It is impossible for those who have once been enlightened, who have tasted the heavenly gift, who have shared in the Holy Spirit, who have tasted the goodness of the word of God and the powers of the coming age, if they fall away, to be brought back to repentance, because to their loss they are crucifying the Son of God all over again and subjecting him to public disgrace."

Read that slowly. The author is describing people who have experienced real spiritual blessings. They were "enlightened," meaning they received the light of the gospel. They "tasted the heavenly gift," meaning they experienced God's salvation. They "shared in the Holy Spirit." They "tasted the goodness of the word of God and the powers of the coming age." These aren't people who casually visited a church once. These are people deep inside the community of faith who experienced God's power firsthand.

And the author says that if such people "fall away," it is impossible to bring them back. Why? Because by walking away from Jesus, they are essentially doing what the people who crucified him did. They are looking at the Son of God and saying, "He's not worth following. His sacrifice doesn't matter. I'm done with him." They are "crucifying the Son of God all over again" and holding him up to public shame.

This is not about someone who struggles with doubt. It's not about someone who sins and feels terrible about it. It's not about someone who goes through a hard season and wonders if God is real. The author is describing a deliberate, final, public rejection of Jesus by someone who has seen and experienced the truth and decided to walk away permanently. The person who worries, "Have I committed this sin?" almost certainly hasn't. The person who has rejected Jesus wouldn't care enough to ask.

The author drives his point home with a picture from farming. Land that receives rain and produces a good crop gets God's blessing. But land that receives the same rain and produces nothing but thorns and thistles is "worthless and in danger of being cursed. In the end it will be burned."

Notice that both parcels of land receive the same rain. God's grace falls on everyone in the community of faith. The question isn't whether you've received it. The question is what you're producing with it. Are you growing? Or are you growing thorns?

The image of "thorns and thistles" would have sent a shiver through anyone who knew their Bible. Those are the exact words from Genesis 3, when God cursed the ground after Adam and Eve's sin. To produce thorns and thistles is to produce the fruit of the curse, to go backward toward the broken world instead of forward toward the restored one. And "burned" is the ultimate fate of a field that has wasted every drop of rain it received.

This is the author's most intense warning yet. It's more pointed than the drifting warning in chapter 2 and more graphic than the wilderness-generation warning in chapters 3–4. He's not trying to terrify his readers into despair. He's trying to shake them awake before they slide any further. The path from spiritual laziness to apostasy isn't as long as people think. Dullness becomes indifference. Indifference becomes neglect. Neglect becomes a hardened heart. And a hardened heart can become a heart that walks away for good.

BETTER THINGS FOR YOU

But the author doesn't leave his readers in the dark. Just when the warning has reached its sharpest edge, he pivots. "Even though we speak like this, dear friends, we are confident of better things in your case, things that have to do with salvation."

"Dear friends." That's the only time in the entire letter he uses that word. After everything he's just said, after the searing imagery of thorns and fire and re-crucifying the Son of God, he calls them "beloved." He pulls them close. He's been a surgeon cutting to save a life, and now he sets down the scalpel and takes their hand.

He tells them he's confident about them. Not because they're perfect, but because he can see the evidence. "God is not unjust; he will not forget your work and the love you have shown him as you have helped his people and continue to help them."

Their faith has been producing fruit. They've served other believers. They've shown love. They've helped people. And God doesn't forget that kind of faithfulness. The rain that fell on their lives has been producing a crop, not thorns. That's evidence that they belong to the "better things" category, not the cursed-land category.

But the author isn't content to just reassure them. He wants more for them. "We want each of you to show this same diligence to the very end, in order to make your hope sure. We do not want you to become lazy, but to imitate those who through faith and patience inherit what has been promised."

There's that word again: lazy. Or "sluggish," the same word he used back in 5:11 when he said they were "slow to learn." The great enemy of the Christian life, according to the author of Hebrews, isn't persecution or temptation or intellectual doubt. It's laziness. It's the slow slide into not caring. It's the decision to coast instead of climb.

The antidote? Diligence. Keep going. Keep serving. Keep paying attention to God's word. And imitate the people who have gone before you, the ones who held on to God's promises through faith and patience until they received what God had promised. The author is about to tell his readers about the greatest example of that kind of faith: Abraham. And after that, he's going to show them a whole cloud of witnesses who lived and died trusting God's promises.

But the immediate point is simple: don't be lazy. Don't stop. The finish line is ahead, and everything God has promised is waiting for those who keep running.

WHAT THIS MEANS FOR US

First, spiritual growth is not optional. The author of Hebrews doesn't treat maturity as a nice goal for overachievers. He treats it as the normal expectation for every believer. If you're not growing, you're in danger. There is no neutral gear in the Christian life. You're either pressing forward or sliding back.

Second, you can lose ground you've already gained. These readers once understood more than they do now. They had moved past the basics, and then they regressed. That's a warning for anyone who thinks past spiritual experiences are enough. What you knew last year doesn't sustain you if you're not growing this year.

Third, the warning is real, but it's not aimed at the anxious. If you're worried about whether you've committed the unforgivable sin, the fact that you're worried is strong evidence that you haven't. The people described in Hebrews 6 aren't losing sleep over their spiritual condition. They've stopped caring. The warning exists to keep people from reaching that point, not to torment people who are still fighting to believe.

Fourth, evidence of real faith is visible. The author's confidence in his readers wasn't based on a feeling. It was based on what he could see: their love, their service, their care for other believers. Real faith produces fruit. If you want to know whether your faith is genuine, look at what it's producing in how you treat other people.

Fifth, laziness is more dangerous than you think. The author treats spiritual sluggishness as a path toward destruction. It doesn't look dramatic. It doesn't feel like rebellion. It just feels like not caring anymore. But "not caring" is the first step on a road that leads somewhere no one wants to go. Fight it. Stay awake. Keep showing up.

TALKING POINTS

1. **The author says his readers should be "teachers" by now but instead need to be re-taught the basics.** What does spiritual growth look like for someone your age? How can you tell if you're growing or stagnating?

2. **The warning in Hebrews 6:4–6 describes people who "fall away" after experiencing real spiritual blessings. But many Christians go through seasons of doubt, struggle, or discouragement without abandoning their faith entirely.** What's the difference between struggling with faith and the kind of "falling away" this passage describes? Why is it important to understand that difference?

3. **The author uses the image of land that receives rain but produces thorns instead of fruit.** What "rain" has God poured into your life? What kind of crop is it producing?

4. **After his harshest warning, the author calls his readers "dear friends" and tells them he's confident about them.** Why do you think he paired such a severe warning with such

warm encouragement? How do warning and encouragement work together?

5. **The author says the antidote to falling away is diligence, not laziness.** What does spiritual diligence look like in everyday life? What are specific things you could do this week to fight spiritual laziness?

The author has said what needed to be said. He's shamed his readers for their sluggishness. He's warned them about the cliff at the end of the road they're walking. And then he's pulled them close, told them he believes in them, and pointed them toward the people whose faith and patience they should imitate.

Now he's ready to get back to the teaching they need. The solid food. The high priesthood of Jesus in the order of Melchizedek. It's the truth that will anchor their souls and carry them through the storm. And it starts with the most mysterious figure in the book of Genesis.

Turn the page.

6

THE PRIEST WHO NEVER STOPS

One of my favorite books growing up was Jules Verne's *Around the World in Eighty Days*. In the story, Phileas Fogg makes a wager that seems impossible. He bets that he can circle the entire globe in eighty days, a feat that everyone around him considers absurd. Throughout the journey, obstacle after obstacle threatens to derail him. Storms. Missed connections. Arrests. Rescues that cost precious time. At multiple points, his traveling companion Passepartout is convinced they've failed. But Fogg keeps going. He never panics. He never quits. And right at the moment when it looks like all hope is lost, he discovers that they've actually gained a day by traveling east. He wins the bet. The promise is kept.

What makes the story work is the absolute certainty that Fogg will honor his word. His entire reputation is staked on the wager. He doesn't say "I'll try." He says "I will." And then he does it, no matter what stands in the way.

The God of the Bible doesn't make wagers. He makes promises. And in Hebrews 6:13–7:28, the author shows his readers that God's promises are backed by something far more reliable than a gentleman's honor. They are backed by an oath

God swore on his own name, and by a High Priest whose very nature guarantees that what God promised will come true.

This is where the author finally delivers the teaching he's been promising since chapter 5. The solid food. The deep truth about who Jesus is as a priest "in the order of Melchizedek." And it changes everything.

GOD'S UNBREAKABLE OATH

The chapter begins not with Melchizedek but with Abraham, because before you can trust a priest, you need to trust the God who appointed him.

When God made his promise to Abraham, he did something extraordinary. "Since there was no one greater for him to swear by, he swore by himself, saying, 'I will surely bless you and give you many descendants.'" In the ancient world, when people made an oath, they swore by something greater than themselves: by a king, by a temple, by the gods. This added weight to their word. But God has no one greater. So he swore by himself. He staked his own identity, his own character, his own being on the truth of his promise.

And Abraham waited. He waited years for the son God had promised. He endured the heartbreak of Sarah's barrenness. He watched the decades pass. And then, after God gave him Isaac and then asked him to offer that son as a sacrifice, Abraham obeyed. God provided a ram instead, and then confirmed his promise with an oath. Abraham "having patiently endured, obtained what was promised."

The author uses this story to make a point about his readers. God gave Abraham two unchangeable things: a promise and an oath. And since it is impossible for God to lie, those two things together create absolute certainty. The readers of Hebrews can have what the author calls "strong encouragement," because the God who promised them salvation is the same God who cannot break his word.

Then comes an image that has comforted believers for two thousand years: "We have this hope as an anchor for the soul, firm and secure."

An anchor keeps a ship from drifting. The readers have been warned about drifting since chapter 2. Now the author tells them what prevents it: hope rooted in the unbreakable promises of God. But this isn't an ordinary anchor dragging along the ocean floor. It reaches upward. It enters "the inner sanctuary behind the curtain, where our forerunner, Jesus, has entered on our behalf."

If you remember the tabernacle from Exodus, the "inner sanctuary behind the curtain" was the Most Holy Place, the room where God's presence dwelt above the ark of the covenant. Only the high priest could enter, and only once a year. It was the holiest spot on earth. The author is saying that the anchor of the Christian's soul is fastened not to anything in this world but to the very throne room of God. Jesus has gone ahead, through the heavens, into God's presence, and he holds us there. The storm can rage all it wants. The anchor holds because it's fastened to something that cannot be shaken.

And the author calls Jesus something no one ever called Aaron: a "forerunner." That word means someone who goes ahead so that others can follow. Aaron entered the Most Holy Place alone. No one could follow him in. But Jesus entered as a forerunner, which means the way is open for his people to come after him.

And the author adds one final phrase to this picture: Jesus has entered as a high priest "forever, in the order of Melchizedek." The mysterious name is back. And now, at last, it's time to explain what it means.

THE MYSTERY OF MELCHIZEDEK

If you've read *What Is the Book of Genesis?*, you might remember a brief, strange scene from Genesis 14. Abraham had just rescued his nephew Lot from a coalition of kings. He was returning from battle when a man named Melchizedek appeared. He's called "king of Salem" and "priest of God Most High." He brought bread and wine, blessed Abraham, and Abraham gave him a tenth of everything he had captured.

Then Melchizedek disappeared from the story. No introduction. No backstory. No mention of his parents, his birth, or his death. He walked into the narrative, blessed the father of God's people, and walked back out.

The author of Hebrews sees something extraordinary in this. He notices that the name "Melchizedek" means "king of righteousness" and that "Salem" means "peace." So this man was both king of righteousness and king of peace. He also notices what the Genesis text *doesn't* say. It gives no record of Melchizedek's father, mother, genealogy, birth, or death. In a book obsessed with genealogies and family lines, this silence is deafening.

The author interprets this silence as deliberate. Melchizedek appears in Genesis as a figure "without beginning of days or end of life." He's described in a way that makes him look like someone who simply exists, without origin or ending. And the author says this was intentional: Melchizedek was "made like the Son of God" and "remains a priest forever."

This doesn't mean Melchizedek was actually divine. It means that the way Genesis presents him creates a portrait that foreshadows the eternal Son. Melchizedek is like a sketch that anticipates the finished painting. The real eternal priest is Jesus. Melchizedek was the preview.

GREATER THAN THE LEVITICAL PRIESTS

But the author doesn't stop at the portrait. He uses the Genesis encounter to prove something his readers might not expect: Melchizedek was greater than the entire Levitical priesthood.

How? Two ways. First, Abraham gave Melchizedek a tithe, a tenth of everything. In the law of Moses, the Levitical priests collected tithes from the people. But Abraham, the ancestor of *all* the Levitical priests, gave a tithe to Melchizedek. That means Melchizedek outranked the entire priestly system that wouldn't even exist for centuries. As the author puts it, you might even say that Levi himself, still unborn in Abraham's body, paid tithes to Melchizedek through his ancestor.

Second, Melchizedek blessed Abraham. And the author states a principle that his readers would have accepted without argument: "The lesser is blessed by the greater." Abraham was the greatest patriarch in Israel's history, the one who carried God's promises. And Melchizedek blessed him. That puts Melchizedek above Abraham and therefore above everyone descended from Abraham, including every priest who ever served in the tabernacle or temple.

The point is devastating for anyone clinging to the old priestly system. Melchizedek was greater than Aaron. And if the priest "in the order of Melchizedek" is greater than Melchizedek's preview, then Jesus stands immeasurably above every priest Israel ever had.

A DIFFERENT KIND OF PRIEST

Now the author asks the question that drives the rest of the chapter: "If perfection could have been attained through the Levitical priesthood, why was there still need for another priest to come, one in the order of Melchizedek, not in the order of Aaron?"

The answer is simple and earth-shaking. The old system didn't work. Not because it was bad, but because it was limited. The priests were mortal. They sinned. They died and had to be replaced. Their sacrifices had to be repeated endlessly. The whole system could manage sin but never master it. It could cover the problem but never cure it.

And so God promised a different kind of priest. Not from the tribe of Levi but from Judah. Not appointed by a law of physical descent but by "the power of an indestructible life." Not temporary but forever. Not established by a mere regulation but by an oath God swore and will never take back.

The author lines up the contrasts like a courtroom lawyer building an unassailable case. The old priests served under a law. Jesus serves under an oath. The old priests were many, because death kept ending their service. Jesus is one, because he "remains forever." The old priests had to offer sacrifices for their own sins before they could help anyone else. Jesus had no sin. He offered himself, once, and sat down.

The key word is "indestructible." The old priests' lives were very destructible. They got sick. They aged. They died. But the life that powers Jesus' priesthood is the eternal life of God himself. It cannot be damaged, diminished, or ended. And because his life is indestructible, his priesthood is "inviolable," a word that means permanent, unchangeable, absolute. No one can take it from him. No one can replace him. No one needs to.

HE SAVES COMPLETELY

In Victor Hugo's *Les Misérables*, the character Jean Valjean is rescued by a single act of extraordinary grace. A bishop gives him silver candlesticks after Valjean has stolen from him, covering Valjean's crime and giving him a new start. That one act changes the entire trajectory of Valjean's life. But here's what makes it even more powerful: the bishop doesn't just help Valjean once and disappear. The memory of that grace sustains Valjean for the rest of his life. It carries him through prison, through poverty, through years of hiding. One act of grace with permanent consequences.

Jesus' priesthood works the same way, except it's not a memory. It's a living, active, present reality. The author reaches the summit of his argument with one of the most powerful verses in the entire letter: "Therefore he is able to save completely those who come to God through him, because he always lives to intercede for them."

Save *completely*. Not partially. Not temporarily. Not "for now." The priest with the indestructible life can save to the absolute fullest extent. He saves so completely that his people are able to persevere until the end and receive everything

God has promised. And the reason he can do this is that "he always lives." Right now, at this very moment, the Son of God is alive at the right hand of the Father, representing his people, sustaining them, interceding for them. He doesn't take breaks. He doesn't retire. He doesn't die and get replaced by someone less qualified.

The chapter closes with a portrait of this High Priest that reads almost like a hymn: "holy, blameless, pure, set apart from sinners, exalted above the heavens." He doesn't need to offer daily sacrifices the way the old priests did. He offered one sacrifice, himself, once for all. And the law appointed weak human beings as high priests. But the oath, which came after the law, appointed "the Son, who has been made perfect forever."

That last phrase, "a Son perfected forever," is the author's final word on the subject before he plunges into the full explanation of what Jesus did. The eternal Son, through his obedient life and sacrificial death, was fully equipped as the Savior of God's people. He is perfect for the job. Forever.

WHAT THIS MEANS FOR US

First, God's promises are as reliable as God himself. When everything in your life feels uncertain, the promises of God are not. He backed them with his own oath and his own character. If God cannot lie, and he swore on his own name, then what he has promised you will happen.

Second, your hope has an anchor. The image of an anchor reaching into the heavenly sanctuary is one of the most powerful in the entire Bible. Your security doesn't depend on how strong your faith feels on any given day. It depends on where the anchor is fastened, and it's fastened to the throne of God through Jesus Christ.

Third, Jesus' priesthood never expires. Every human system breaks down eventually. Leaders retire, institutions fail, and even the best human helpers can only do so much. But the priest who holds your salvation has an indestructible life. He will never burn out, give up, or be replaced. He is always there, always alive, always interceding.

Fourth, "save completely" means what it says. Jesus doesn't save halfway. He doesn't get you started and leave you to finish on your own. He saves to the fullest possible extent, providing everything you need to persevere from now until the end. If you come to God through him, his ability to save you is unlimited.

Fifth, the old has given way to the better. The Levitical priesthood wasn't bad. It was God-given. But it was a shadow of something far greater. Everything it pointed to has arrived in Jesus. Clinging to the shadow when the reality has come makes no sense. The better covenant, the better hope, the better priest, they are all here. They are all his.

TALKING POINTS

1. **God swore an oath to Abraham because he wanted his people to be absolutely certain of his promises.** What makes it hard for you to trust God's promises? How does knowing that God backed his word with his own character change the way you think about your future?

2. **The author calls hope an "anchor for the soul."** What does that image mean to you? How is an anchor that reaches into heaven different from the way most people think about security?

3. **Melchizedek had no recorded beginning or end, which made him a picture of the eternal Son.** Why do you think God included this mysterious figure in Genesis? What does it teach us about how the whole Bible points to Jesus?

4. **The old priests died and had to be replaced. Jesus "remains forever."** What difference does it make in your daily life to know that your High Priest never changes, never weakens, and never stops serving on your behalf?

5. **Hebrews 7:25 says Jesus is able to "save completely" those who come to God through him.** What does "completely" mean to you? How does this verse encourage you when you feel like your faith isn't strong enough?

The author of Hebrews has built his case carefully, layer by layer. He's shown that God's promises are certain. He's shown that Melchizedek foreshadowed a priest greater than Aaron. He's shown that the old system was limited and that Jesus, the eternal Son, has replaced it with a priesthood powered by indestructible life. He's shown that this priest saves completely and intercedes forever.

Now comes the payoff. The author is about to take his readers inside the heavenly sanctuary itself and show them what Jesus actually did there. The sacrifice. The covenant. The once-for-all offering that changed everything.

Turn the page.

7

ONCE FOR ALL

Have you ever watched a scene in a movie where someone tries the same thing over and over and it never works? In *Despicable Me 2*, there's a running gag where characters keep attempting the same approach to a problem, each time with the same disastrous result. It's funny on screen. But imagine if it were serious. Imagine someone trying to bail water out of a sinking boat with a cup that has a hole in it. They scoop and pour, scoop and pour, faster and faster, but the water keeps coming because the cup can't hold it. That's what the old sacrificial system looked like from God's perspective. The priests kept offering, year after year, the same sacrifices that could never actually solve the problem.

In *A Tale of Two Cities*, Charles Dickens gives us one of the most famous openings in all of literature: "It was the best of times, it was the worst of times." But the real power of the novel comes at the end, when Sydney Carton takes the place of Charles Darnay at the guillotine. Carton, a wasted, directionless man, gives his life so that Darnay can live. It's a substitution. One dies so another can go free. And Carton's final words echo through the centuries: "It is a far, far better thing that I do, than I have ever done." One man. One act. One death that changes everything.

Hebrews 8:1–10:18 is the theological center of the entire letter, and it tells a story that makes Carton's sacrifice look like a shadow of something infinitely greater. This is where the author explains what Jesus actually *did* as our High Priest. Not in theory. Not in metaphor. This is the full picture of the sacrifice that ended all sacrifices, the covenant that replaced the old one, and the reason why Jesus sat down when every priest before him had to keep standing.

THE MAIN POINT

The author announces his main point at the very beginning: "Now the main point of what we are saying is this: We do have such a high priest, who sat down at the right hand of the throne of the Majesty in heaven, and who serves in the sanctuary, the true tabernacle set up by the Lord, not by a mere human being."

Everything the author has been building toward since chapter 1 converges here. We have a High Priest. He has sat down, meaning his work is complete. He is at the right hand of God, meaning he holds the highest authority in the universe. And he serves in the true sanctuary, not the earthly tent Moses built in the wilderness, but heaven itself, the place where God actually dwells.

God gave Moses a detailed blueprint for building the tabernacle, and the text says Moses had to follow the pattern exactly. The author of Hebrews now explains why: the earthly tabernacle was a copy. A model. A shadow of the real thing. The real sanctuary was always in heaven. The earthly one existed so that God's people could understand, in a way they could see and touch, what God was preparing in a realm they couldn't see. Every piece of furniture, every ritual, every curtain was a preview of a heavenly reality that would one day be revealed through Jesus.

This matters because if the sanctuary was a copy, then the sacrifices offered in it were also copies. Previews. Shadows. They were real and God-given, but they were pointing to something greater. The author is about to show what that something greater is.

THE NEW COVENANT PROMISE

But first, he introduces the new covenant. And he does it by quoting one of the longest Old Testament passages found anywhere in the New Testament: Jeremiah 31:31–34.

Centuries before Jesus was born, God told the prophet Jeremiah that the old covenant, the one made at Mount Sinai, was going to be replaced. Not because God made a mistake, but because the people couldn't keep their end of it. "They did not remain faithful to my covenant," God said, "and I turned away from them." The problem wasn't the covenant itself. The problem was the human heart. The people kept breaking their promises. The system of sacrifices could manage the symptoms, but it couldn't cure the disease.

So God promised something radically new. "I will put my laws in their minds and write them on their hearts. I will be their God, and they will be my people. No longer will they teach their neighbor, saying, 'Know the Lord,' because they will all know me, from the least of them to the greatest. For I will forgive their wickedness and will remember their sins no more."

Four promises. Laws written on hearts instead of stone tablets. A direct, personal knowledge of God available to everyone. Complete forgiveness of sin. And the most staggering of all: God would *remember their sins no more.*

The author of Hebrews draws a devastating conclusion from Jeremiah's prophecy: "By calling this covenant 'new,' God has made the first one obsolete; and what is obsolete and outdated will soon disappear." The old covenant wasn't permanent. It was never meant to be. It was a placeholder, designed to prepare God's people for the real thing.

THE LIMITS OF THE OLD SYSTEM

Now the author takes his readers inside the old tabernacle one last time, and it's clear he wants them to see how limited it really was.

He describes the layout: the outer room, called the Holy Place, with its lampstand and table and bread. Behind the curtain, the inner room, the Most Holy Place, with the gold-covered ark of the covenant containing the stone tablets, Aaron's staff, and a jar of manna. Above the ark, the cherubim overshadowing the mercy seat.

The arrangement itself told a story. The outer room was accessible to the priests every day. But the inner room, the Most Holy Place, was off-limits to everyone except the high priest, and he could enter only once a year, on the Day of Atonement. And he couldn't enter empty-handed. He brought blood, offered first for his own sins and then for the sins of the people.

The author says the Holy Spirit was making a point through this arrangement: "The way into the Most Holy Place had not yet been disclosed as long as the first tabernacle was still functioning." In other words, the very structure of the tabernacle was a confession that the problem hadn't been solved yet. The curtain was still there. The barrier was still up. Access to God's full presence was still restricted.

The old sacrifices were "not able to clear the conscience of the worshiper." They dealt with external rituals, with "food and drink and various ceremonial washings, external regulations applying until the time of the new order." They kept the system running, but they couldn't change the person on the inside. They couldn't reach the heart.

INTO THE TRUE SANCTUARY

Then comes the moment the whole letter has been building toward. "But when Christ came as high priest of the good things that are now already here, he went through the greater and more perfect tabernacle that is not made with human hands, that is to say, is not a part of this creation. He did not enter by means of the blood of goats and calves; but he entered the Most Holy Place once for all by his own blood, thus obtaining eternal redemption."

Read that slowly. Every word matters. Christ entered the real sanctuary, heaven itself. He didn't bring animal blood. He brought his own. And he entered "once for all," a phrase the author uses like a hammer, driving home the point that this sacrifice never needs to be repeated. It's done. Finished. The redemption he obtained isn't annual. It's eternal.

The author makes a comparison that his original readers would have felt deeply. "The blood of goats and bulls and the ashes of a heifer sprinkled on those who are ceremonially unclean sanctify them so that they are outwardly clean." That was real. The old sacrifices did something. They restored people to ritual cleanness. But then the author raises the stakes immeasurably: "How much more, then, will the blood of Christ, who through the eternal Spirit offered himself unblemished to God, cleanse our consciences from acts that lead to death, so that we may serve the living God!"

Animal blood cleaned the outside. Christ's blood cleans the inside. The conscience. The place where guilt lives. The part of you that knows you've done wrong and can't shake the feeling. The old system could make you ritually acceptable. Christ's sacrifice makes you actually clean, from the inside out, so that you can serve God with a free heart.

THE OBEDIENCE THAT CHANGED EVERYTHING

The author then explains *why* Christ's sacrifice succeeds where animal sacrifices failed. It comes down to obedience. He quotes Psalm 40, placing the words on the lips of Christ as he enters the world: "Sacrifice and offering you did not desire, but a body you prepared for me. With burnt offerings and sin offerings you were not pleased. Then I said, 'Here I am. It is written about me in the scroll. I have come to do your will, O God.'"

This is the heart of everything. God wasn't ultimately satisfied with animal sacrifices. They couldn't solve the problem because an animal has no will to offer. It can't choose obedience. It can't love God. It's just blood. But when the Son of

God took on a human body and lived a life of perfect, willing obedience to the Father, from his first breath to his last, *that* was the offering God had always wanted. Not the blood of an unwilling animal, but the willing surrender of a life lived entirely for God.

The author draws out the implications: "He sets aside the first to establish the second. And by that will, we have been made holy through the sacrifice of the body of Jesus Christ once for all." The old system is set aside. The new one is established. And God's people are made holy, not by repeating rituals year after year, but by the once-for-all offering of Jesus' obedient life and death. "Once for all" means the job is finished so thoroughly that it never needs to be done again.

HE SAT DOWN

The author brings his argument to a breathtaking conclusion by placing the old priests and Jesus side by side one final time. "Day after day every priest stands and performs his religious duties; again and again he offers the same sacrifices, which can never take away sins." Standing. Repeating. Never finishing. That was the old priesthood in a single sentence.

"But when this priest had offered for all time one sacrifice for sins, he sat down at the right hand of God, and since that time he waits for his enemies to be made his footstool. For by one sacrifice he has made perfect forever those who are being made holy."

He sat down. The author has been saying this since the first chapter, and now we finally understand the full weight of it. Jesus sat down because there was nothing left to do. The sacrifice was sufficient. The cleansing was complete. The way into God's presence was open. And from that seated position at God's right hand, Jesus now waits for the final victory while continually sustaining his people with everything they need to persevere.

"By one sacrifice he has made perfect forever those who are being made holy." One sacrifice. Perfect forever. Those two phrases side by side are almost too big to hold. The sacrifice was one, and its effect is forever. There will never be another offering for sin because there will never need to be.

The author closes by returning to Jeremiah. The Holy Spirit testifies: "Their sins and lawless acts I will remember no more." And then the final sentence of this great section: "And where these have been forgiven, sacrifice for sin is no longer necessary."

It's over. The case is closed. The need for sacrifice has ended because the one sacrifice that actually works has been offered.

WHAT THIS MEANS FOR US

First, the old was a shadow; Christ is the reality. Everything in the tabernacle system, the sacrifices, the priests, the curtain, the ark, all of it was pointing to Jesus. When you read Exodus and Leviticus, you're reading the preview. When you read Hebrews, you're seeing the finished work those previews anticipated.

Second, Christ's sacrifice changes you from the inside. The old system could make you outwardly clean. Christ's blood cleanses your conscience. That means the guilt, the shame, the nagging sense that you're not good enough, all of it can be addressed by what Jesus did. You don't have to carry it anymore.

Third, God's new covenant writes his will on your heart. Under the old covenant, the law was on stone tablets, external and distant. Under the new, God puts his desires inside you. He doesn't just tell you what to do. He gives you a new heart that *wants* to do it. That's the transformation the old system could never provide.

Fourth, "once for all" means you can stop trying to earn it. If the sacrifice is complete and the forgiveness is real, then you don't need to keep performing in order to be accepted. Jesus sat down because the work was done. You can rest in what he accomplished instead of exhausting yourself trying to add to it.

Fifth, God remembers your sins no more. This isn't divine amnesia. It's a deliberate choice. God, through the sacrifice of his Son, has decided not to hold your sins against you. They don't define your relationship with him anymore. The record is clean. That's the promise of the new covenant, and it's backed by the blood of Jesus.

TALKING POINTS

1. **The earthly tabernacle was a copy of the heavenly one.** What does it mean that God gave Moses a "shadow" to build rather than the real thing? How does knowing the original plan was always heavenly change the way you think about worship?

2. **The old sacrifices couldn't "clear the conscience of the worshiper."** What's the difference between being outwardly clean and having a clean conscience? Why does the inside matter more?

3. **Jesus quoted Psalm 40 to say that God wasn't ultimately pleased with animal sacrifices but wanted obedience.**

Why is a willing, obedient life more valuable to God than the blood of animals? What does this teach us about what God really wants from us?

4. **The author keeps saying "once for all."** Why is it so important that Christ's sacrifice never needs to be repeated? How is this different from the way the old system worked, and what does it mean for you personally?

5. **God promises in the new covenant to "remember their sins no more."** How does this promise make you feel? Is it hard to believe that God doesn't hold your past against you? What would change in your life if you truly believed this?

The author has finished the theological heart of his letter. He has shown his readers a High Priest seated at God's right hand, a sacrifice offered once for all, a covenant that transforms from the inside, and a God who has chosen to forget their sins. Everything the Old Testament was reaching for, Jesus accomplished. The shadow has given way to the substance. The copy has been replaced by the original. The need for any further sacrifice has been permanently, irreversibly, gloriously ended.

Now comes the question: What do you do with all of this? How do you live in light of a sacrifice this complete, a High Priest this sufficient, and a covenant this generous? The author is about to tell his readers, and the answer will carry them through the rest of the letter.

Turn the page.

8

NOW WHAT?

In *The Count of Monte Cristo*, Alexandre Dumas tells the story of Edmond Dantès, a young sailor who is falsely imprisoned for fourteen years in a dark island fortress. During those years, a fellow prisoner named Abbé Faria teaches him everything: languages, science, history, swordsmanship. Faria also reveals the location of an enormous hidden treasure on the island of Monte Cristo. When Dantès finally escapes, he finds the treasure. He becomes the wealthiest man in Europe. He has resources beyond anything he could have imagined.

But having the treasure isn't the end of the story. It's the beginning. The entire second half of the novel is about what Dantès *does* with what he's been given. Will he use it for justice or revenge? For generosity or cruelty? The treasure changes everything, but only if he acts on it.

In *Toy Story 4*, Woody spends the whole movie trying to figure out who he is now that his kid doesn't need him the way he used to. He has everything he needs. He has friends. He has purpose. He has a new owner who loves him. But the question that drives the story isn't "What do you have?" It's "What are you going to do with it?"

That's exactly where the author of Hebrews stands at the beginning of Hebrews 10:19. He has just finished the theological heart of his letter. He has shown his readers who Jesus is, what he did as High Priest, how his sacrifice was offered once for all, and why the new covenant replaces the old. The treasure has been laid out in full.

Now comes the question that will drive the rest of the letter: What are you going to do with all of this?

THREE THINGS TO DO

The author begins with a summary of everything he's been teaching, boiled down to two privileges his readers now possess. First, they have "confidence to enter the Most Holy Place by the blood of Jesus, by a new and living way opened for us through the curtain." Second, they have "a great priest over the house of God."

If you've been following this letter, you know the weight of those two statements. Under the old system, only one person could enter the Most Holy Place, only once a year, only with the blood of an animal, and only after offering a sacrifice for his own sins first. Now every believer has the right to walk straight into God's presence at any time, through the sacrifice of Jesus, who opened a way that is both "new" (it didn't exist before) and "living" (it will never grow old or obsolete). The curtain that once kept people out has been transformed into a doorway by the flesh and blood of Jesus.

And standing in that heavenly sanctuary, representing his people before the Father, is their great priest, the Son of God himself.

With those two realities in place, the author issues three commands that cover the entire Christian life. They correspond to the three great virtues of faith, hope, and love.

"Let us draw near to God with a sincere heart and with the full assurance that faith brings, having our hearts sprinkled to cleanse us from a guilty conscience and having our bodies washed with pure water."

That's the first command: draw near. Come to God. Don't stay at a distance. Don't treat the throne of grace like something you might visit someday. Come now. Come often. Come with a sincere heart and with full confidence that you're welcome, because Jesus' sacrifice has dealt with your guilt. The old system left people standing outside. The new way invites them in.

"Let us hold unswervingly to the hope we profess, for he who promised is faithful."

That's the second: hold on to hope. Don't let go of what you believe about the future. The God who promised you an eternal inheritance is faithful. He doesn't break promises. He doesn't forget. He doesn't change his mind. Whatever pressure the world puts on you to give up or compromise, the promise of God is more real and more durable than anything you can see with your eyes.

"And let us consider how we may spur one another on toward love and good deeds, not giving up meeting together, as some are in the habit of doing, but encouraging each other, and all the more as you see the Day approaching."

That's the third: take care of each other. The Christian life was never designed to be lived alone. The author has been concerned about isolation since chapter 3, when he told his readers to "encourage one another daily." Now he gets specific. Some of them have stopped showing up. They've pulled away from the church. Maybe they're afraid of being associated with a persecuted group. Maybe they've just gotten lazy. Either way, the author says it has to stop. They need each other, and the need is getting more urgent, not less, as "the Day" of Christ's return draws closer.

These three commands are the author's answer to the question "Now what?" Draw near to God. Hold on to hope. Take care of each other. Faith, hope, and love. Everything else the author says in the rest of the letter flows from these three.

A SECOND WARNING

But the author knows his readers. He knows that some of them are drifting, and he knows where drifting leads. So immediately after this beautiful invitation, he drops the most severe warning in the entire letter. "If we deliberately keep on sinning after we have received the knowledge of the truth, no sacrifice for sins is left, but only a fearful expectation of judgment and of raging fire that will consume the enemies of God."

This is not about someone who struggles with sin and keeps repenting. The word "deliberately" and the phrase "keep on sinning" point to something far more serious: a willful, ongoing, public rejection of the salvation Jesus provides. The author is describing someone who has heard the full truth about Christ's sacrifice and then walks away from it on purpose, with no intention of coming back.

And his point is devastating in its logic. If the sacrifice of Jesus is the only sacrifice that actually works, and if that sacrifice has been offered once for all and never needs to be repeated, then what happens to someone who rejects it? There's nothing left. No backup plan. No second sacrifice. No plan B. If you walk away from the only thing that can save you, there is nothing between you and judgment.

The author makes his case by comparison. Under the law of Moses, if someone rejected God's covenant and was convicted by two or three witnesses, that person was executed without mercy. The stakes were life and death. Then the author raises the stakes infinitely higher: "How much more severely do you think someone deserves to be punished who has trampled the Son of God underfoot, who has treated as an unholy thing the blood of the covenant that sanctified them, and who has insulted the Spirit of grace?"

Three descriptions of the apostate, each worse than the last. "Trampled the Son of God underfoot" means treating the exalted one, the radiance of God's glory, the heir of all things, as if he were worthless. "Treated as unholy the blood of the covenant" means looking at the sacrifice that cleansed your sin and calling it common, ordinary, meaningless. "Insulted the Spirit of grace" means rejecting with arrogant contempt the very presence of God in your life.

The author wants his readers to feel revulsion at this description. He wants them to say, "That's not me. I would never do that." And that's exactly the point. The warning isn't meant to describe them. It's meant to keep them from ever becoming the person it describes.

He closes the warning with two Old Testament quotations: "It is mine to avenge; I will repay," and "The Lord will judge his people." And then one of the most sobering sentences in the entire Bible: "It is a dreadful thing to fall into the hands of the living God."

The God who is "living" is the God who acts. He is the God who keeps promises, who judges sin, who vindicates his people. To fall into his hands as someone who has rejected his mercy is terrifying beyond words. But to fall into his hands as someone who has trusted his Son is the safest place in the universe. Everything depends on which side you're standing on.

REMEMBER WHO YOU ARE

After that warning, the author does something he's done before. He pulls his readers close and reminds them that they are not the people he just described.

"Remember those earlier days after you had received the light, when you endured in a great conflict full of suffering. Sometimes you were publicly exposed to insult and persecution; at other times you stood side by side with those who were so treated. You suffered along with those in prison and joyfully accepted the confiscation of your property, because you knew that you yourselves had better and lasting possessions."

This is remarkable. These readers weren't always drifting. There was a time, right after their conversion, when they stood firm under incredible pressure. They were publicly humiliated. They were insulted. They were robbed of their property. Some of their friends were thrown in prison, and instead of distancing themselves, they visited them, knowing it could cost them everything. And they did all of this with joy, because they believed they had something better waiting for them, something the world couldn't take away.

The author is holding up a mirror: "This is who you were. This is who you still are. Don't throw that away."

"So do not throw away your confidence; it will be richly rewarded. You need to persevere so that when you have done the will of God, you will receive what he has promised."

The word "confidence" here is the same word used earlier for the right of access to God's presence. It's not just a feeling. It's a God-given privilege. And the reward attached to it is enormous: everything God has promised, the eternal inheritance, the heavenly homeland, the unshakable kingdom. But it requires perseverance. It requires doing the will of God not just on the good days, but on the days when the cost feels unbearable.

THE COMING ONE WILL COME

The author closes this section by quoting the prophet Habakkuk, and in doing so, he sets up everything that will follow in the next two chapters. "For, 'In just a little while, he who is coming will come and will not delay.' And, 'But my righteous one will live by faith. And I take no pleasure in the one who shrinks back.'"

Two kinds of people. Two destinies. The righteous person lives by faith, trusting God's promises even when the fulfillment seems far away. The person who shrinks back faces God's displeasure. The readers must choose which group they belong to.

The author makes his choice for them: "But we do not belong to those who shrink back and are destroyed, but to those who have faith and are saved." That sentence is a bridge. It looks backward at everything the author has said about Christ's sacrifice and forward to everything he's about to say about the life of faith. It's a declaration: we are not the quitters. We are not the ones who drift away. We are the people of faith.

And in the very next chapter, the author will show them what that kind of faith looks like by introducing a parade of witnesses who lived it.

WHAT THIS MEANS FOR US

First, access to God is a privilege to be used, not admired. The author doesn't describe the open way into God's presence so his readers can feel good about it. He describes it so they'll actually walk through it. Prayer, worship, honest confession, daily dependence on God: these aren't extras. They're the means of survival for people living in a hostile world.

Second, community is not optional. Some of the original readers had stopped meeting together. The author treats this as a serious problem, not a minor preference. You cannot hold on to hope alone. You cannot "spur one another on toward love" if you never see each other. Isolation is one of the most effective tools the enemy has for destroying faith.

Third, the warning is real and the comfort is real. The author doesn't soften the warning about apostasy, and he doesn't withhold the encouragement about his readers' faithfulness. Both are true at the same time. The warning keeps you from presumption. The encouragement keeps you from despair. Together, they produce the perseverance that leads to life.

Fourth, your past faithfulness is evidence of your real identity. When the author reminds his readers of their earlier courage, he's not indulging in nostalgia. He's showing them proof that their faith is genuine. If you've ever suffered for doing the right thing and kept going anyway, that's not a memory to discard. It's evidence that you belong to the people who have faith and are saved.

Fifth, the "coming one" will come. The author's final word in this section is about the future. Christ will return. The wait may feel long. The pressure may feel unbearable. But the one who is coming will not delay. Everything God has promised is on its way. Your job is to keep the faith until it arrives.

TALKING POINTS

1. **The author gives three commands: draw near, hold fast, and encourage each other.** Which of these three do you find most difficult right now? Why?
2. **Some of the original readers had stopped meeting with other Christians.** Why do you think people pull away from Christian community? What are the dangers of trying to live the faith alone?
3. **The warning in 10:26–31 describes someone who "deliberately keeps on sinning" after knowing the truth.** How is this different from a Christian who struggles with sin but keeps coming back to God? Why is it important to understand the difference?
4. **The author reminds his readers of a time when they joyfully accepted the loss of their property because they believed they had "better and lasting possessions."** What would it take for you to have that kind of joy in the face of loss? What are the "better and lasting possessions" that make earthly losses bearable?

5. **The section ends with a choice: shrink back, or live by faith.** What does "living by faith" look like for someone your age? What are the things that tempt you to shrink back?

The author has drawn a line. On one side are the people who shrink back. On the other are the people who live by faith. He has told his readers which side they belong on. He has reminded them of who they were when their faith was fresh and courageous. He has warned them about what happens to those who walk away. And he has pointed them forward to the return of Christ, the ultimate reward for those who endure.

Now he's going to show them what faith looks like in action. Not with abstract theology, but with stories. Real people who trusted God when everything said they shouldn't. A hall of fame stretching from the beginning of creation to the edge of the Promised Land. And standing at the end of that hall, the one who perfected the faith they all practiced.

Turn the page.

9

THE PEOPLE WHO LIVED BY FAITH

Another Jules Verne favorite when I was a kid was *20,000 Leagues Under the Sea*. Verne takes his readers on a journey with characters who must trust what they cannot see. When Professor Aronnax is trapped aboard Captain Nemo's submarine, the Nautilus, he has no way to verify where they are or where they're going. The ocean is invisible from the inside. He can't see the surface. He can't check a map. All he has is a porthole and the word of a captain he barely knows. And yet, day after day, Aronnax makes decisions based on what Nemo tells him is out there, even when the water is dark and the destination is uncertain. He acts on a reality he cannot see.

In *Zootopia*, Judy Hopps leaves her family's carrot farm to become the first rabbit police officer in a city where no one believes she belongs. Her parents don't think she can do it. Her boss doesn't think she can do it. The entire city is designed for animals bigger and stronger than she is. But Judy goes anyway, because she believes in something she can't yet prove: that she was made for this, and that Zootopia can be a place where anyone can be anything. She bets her whole life on a future that doesn't exist yet.

Hebrews 11 is about people like that. Not fictional characters, but real men and women who wagered everything on a God they couldn't see and a future they hadn't received. They left homes, faced armies, endured prisons, and died in deserts because they were convinced that the invisible God was more real than the visible world and that his promises were more certain than anything their eyes could show them.

The author of Hebrews calls them the people who lived "by faith." And he lines them up, one after another, in the most extraordinary roll call in the entire Bible.

WHAT FAITH ACTUALLY IS

Before introducing a single name, the author defines what he means by faith. "Now faith is the reality of things hoped for, the evidence of things not seen." This isn't a sentimental feeling. It's not wishful thinking or positive vibes. Faith, as the author of Hebrews describes it, is living as if the things God has promised are real, even though you can't hold them in your hands yet. It's conducting your life based on the conviction that God's invisible world is more solid than the visible one.

The definition has two parts. First, faith treats "things hoped for" as real. The people in this chapter lived as if the heavenly city, the eternal reward, and God's promised future were already certain. They didn't just hope things would turn out okay. They organized their entire lives around a destination they hadn't reached.

Second, faith is "the evidence of things not seen." The faithful prove God's reality by the way they live. When someone trusts God's power and experiences his faithfulness, that experience becomes evidence. The lives of the people in this chapter are proof that the unseen God is real and active.

And then, before naming anyone, the author makes one more foundational statement: "By faith we understand that the universe was formed at God's command, so that what is seen was not made out of what was visible." Everything begins here. The visible world was created by an invisible God through his word. If you believe that, then you've already accepted the most basic principle of faith: the unseen is more fundamental than the seen. The God who spoke the stars into existence is more real than the stars themselves.

FROM ABEL TO NOAH

The roll call begins with three men from the earliest chapters of Genesis. Abel offered a sacrifice that God accepted, and through that offering he was declared righteous. He "still speaks, even though he is dead." Abel was the first person in the Bible to demonstrate that living by faith might cost you your life. His brother Cain killed him for it. And yet, through the record of his faith, Abel's witness outlasted his murderer by thousands of years.

Enoch "was taken from this life, so that he did not experience death." He walked with God so faithfully that God simply took him. If Abel shows that faith may lead to suffering without immediate rescue, Enoch shows that God's power can transcend death entirely. Together, they set the pattern for the rest of the chapter: sometimes faith means suffering; sometimes it means deliverance. Always it means trusting the God who holds both in his hands.

Between these two examples, the author drops a verse that might be the most important sentence in the chapter: "Without faith it is impossible to please God, because anyone who comes to him must believe that he exists and that he rewards those who earnestly seek him." Two things are required. You have to believe God is real. And you have to believe he rewards those who pursue him. Without these two convictions, nothing else in this chapter makes sense.

Noah rounds out the opening trio. "By faith Noah, when warned about things not yet seen, in holy fear built an ark to save his family." The flood hadn't started. The sky was clear. But Noah believed God's warning about a future judgment and built an enormous boat on dry land because he trusted the word of the God who spoke it. By that faith, he "condemned the world and became heir of the righteousness that comes by faith." Noah shows that faith trusts God's warnings about the future as much as his promises.

ABRAHAM AND THE PATRIARCHS

If there is a star of this chapter, it's Abraham. The author devotes more space to him than to anyone else, and for good reason. Abraham is the father of God's people, and his life is the clearest picture of what it looks like to live by faith over a long period of time.

"By faith Abraham, when called to go to a place he would later receive as his inheritance, obeyed and went, even though he did not know where he was going." That sentence captures everything. God called. Abraham obeyed. He didn't have a map. He didn't know the destination. He just went. And when he arrived in the land God had promised, he never owned it. He "lived in tents, as did Isaac and Jacob, who were heirs with him of the same promise." He spent his whole life as a foreigner in the place God said would belong to his descendants.

Why? "For he was looking forward to the city with foundations, whose architect and builder is God." Abraham wasn't waiting for a piece of real estate. He was looking for the permanent, eternal city that God himself had designed and built. The land of Canaan was just the place where he camped while he waited for something infinitely better.

By faith, Sarah received the power to have a child even though she was far too old. From that one couple, "as good as dead," came descendants "as numerous as the stars in the sky and as countless as the sand on the seashore."

Then the author pauses and steps back to explain what all of this means. "All these people were still living by faith when they died. They did not receive the things promised; they only saw them and welcomed them from a distance, admitting that they were foreigners and strangers on earth."

This is one of the most important paragraphs in the chapter. The patriarchs died without receiving what God had promised. They never saw the heavenly city. They never entered God's rest. They believed in it, they organized their lives around it, they could see it with the eyes of faith, but they didn't get to hold it. And yet they kept going. They "admitted that they were foreigners and strangers on earth" because they knew this world wasn't their home.

"Instead, they were longing for a better country, a heavenly one. Therefore God is not ashamed to be called their God, for he has prepared a city for them." God is not ashamed. That phrase should stop you in your tracks. The Creator of the universe, the one who spoke the galaxies into existence, looks at these wandering, tent-dwelling, promise-trusting people and says, "I'm proud to be called their God." And the reason is that he has actually prepared the city they were seeking. It's real. Their faith wasn't misplaced.

The Abraham section reaches its peak when the author describes the offering of Isaac. "By faith Abraham, when God tested him, offered Isaac as a sacrifice." Abraham reasoned that "God could even raise the dead." The man who had received his son from a God who gives life trusted that same God to give life again, even after death. Isaac was returned to him, and the author says this was "a symbol" pointing to something even greater: the resurrection of the righteous at the end of the age.

Isaac, Jacob, and Joseph each carry the torch of faith in their own way, all of them blessing the next generation, all of them trusting God's promises about a future they wouldn't live to see.

MOSES AND THE EXODUS

The chapter shifts to Moses, and the tone changes. If Abraham's faith was about patient waiting, Moses' faith is about courageous resistance.

It starts with his parents, who "saw he was no ordinary child" and hid him for three months, defying Pharaoh's order to kill every Hebrew boy. Their faith in God's purposes was stronger than their fear of the king.

Then Moses himself made his choice. "By faith Moses, when he had grown up, refused to be known as the son of

Pharaoh's daughter. He chose to be mistreated along with the people of God rather than to enjoy the fleeting pleasures of sin." He looked at the wealth and power of Egypt, and he looked at the suffering people of God, and he chose the suffering. Why? "He regarded disgrace for the sake of Christ as of greater value than the treasures of Egypt, because he was looking ahead to his reward."

The author calls Moses' suffering "disgrace for the sake of Christ." Moses lived centuries before Jesus, but the author sees a connection: anyone who identifies with God's people and suffers for it is sharing in the reproach that would ultimately fall on Christ himself. Moses endured the same kind of rejection the Son of God would endure, and for the same reason: loyalty to the people and purposes of God.

"By faith he left Egypt, not fearing the king's anger; he persevered because he saw him who is invisible." Moses kept going because he could see, with the eyes of faith, the God who cannot be seen with physical eyes. That's the deepest description of faith in the entire chapter. To see the invisible God and live accordingly.

Then came the great deliverances. By faith, Moses established the Passover. By faith, the people crossed the Red Sea on dry ground. By faith, the walls of Jericho fell. By faith, Rahab the prostitute welcomed the Israelite spies and was saved when everyone else in her city perished. A foreign woman with no claim to God's people chose to identify with them, and her faith preserved her life.

THE UNNAMED FAITHFUL

The author can't stop. The names keep coming, faster now, like a river picking up speed. "And what more shall I say? I do not have time to tell about Gideon, Barak, Samson, Jephthah, David, Samuel and the prophets." He rattles off their accomplishments: they conquered kingdoms, administered justice, shut the mouths of lions, quenched the fury of the flames, escaped the edge of the sword. Women received back their dead, raised to life again.

But then the tone shifts one final, devastating time. "There were others who were tortured, refusing to be released so that they might gain an even better resurrection. Some faced jeers and flogging, and even chains and imprisonment. They were put to death by stoning; they were sawed in two; they were killed by the sword. They went about in sheepskins and goatskins, destitute, persecuted and mistreated. The world was not worthy of them."

Read that last sentence again. "The world was not worthy of them." These were people who had nothing by the world's standards. No homes. No possessions. No safety. They wandered in deserts and mountains, hiding in caves and holes in the ground. And the author of Hebrews says the world didn't deserve to have them.

NOT WITHOUT US

The chapter ends with a statement that ties everything together and points directly at the readers. "These were all commended for their faith, yet none of them received what had been promised, since God had planned something better for us so that only together with us would they be made perfect."

Every person in this chapter, from Abel to the nameless martyrs hiding in caves, lived and died without receiving the final promise. They trusted God. They obeyed. They endured. And they still hadn't entered the heavenly city. Why? Because God's plan included the readers of this letter. It included us. The faithful of old won't be made complete without the faithful who come after them. The whole family enters together, through the one who made it all possible: Jesus.

That's where this chapter is pointing. Every "by faith" in this chapter is a step on a road that leads to the next chapter's opening line: "Let us fix our eyes on Jesus, the pioneer and perfecter of faith."

WHAT THIS MEANS FOR US

First, faith is not a feeling. It's a way of life. Every person in this chapter acted on what they believed. Abraham left home. Moses refused a palace. Rahab hid the spies. Faith without action isn't the kind of faith Hebrews is talking about.

Second, God's faithful don't always get rescued. Abel was murdered. Others were sawed in two. Faith doesn't guarantee a comfortable life. It guarantees that your life has meaning and that your destination is certain, even if the road is brutal.

Third, the world is not your home. Abraham, Isaac, and Jacob "admitted that they were foreigners and strangers on earth." If you feel out of place in a world that doesn't share your values, you're in good company. The greatest people of faith in history felt the same way.

Fourth, God is not ashamed of people who trust him. No matter how small, insignificant, or out of step with the culture you feel, if you are living by faith in God's promises, he is proud to be called your God. And he has prepared a city for you.

Fifth, the story isn't over. The faithful of the past didn't receive the final promise because they were waiting for us. We are part of the same family, the same story, the same pilgrimage. And together, through Jesus, we will reach the city they were seeking.

TALKING POINTS

1. **The author defines faith as "the reality of things hoped for, the evidence of things not seen."** How is this different from the way most people use the word "faith"? What does it look like to live as if God's promises are real when you can't see them yet?

2. **Abraham "obeyed and went, even though he did not know where he was going."** Have you ever had to trust God without knowing how things would turn out? What made it hard? What helped you keep going?

3. **Moses "regarded disgrace for the sake of Christ as of greater value than the treasures of Egypt."** What are the "treasures of Egypt" in your life, the things the world offers that could tempt you away from following God? How do you weigh them against the eternal reward?

4. **The author says "the world was not worthy" of the faithful who suffered without deliverance.** How does this change the way you think about people who seem to lose everything for their faith? What does their story teach you about what really matters?

5. **The chapter ends by saying the faithful of old won't be made perfect "apart from us."** What does it mean to be

part of a story that stretches back to the beginning of creation? How does knowing you're connected to Abel, Abraham, and Moses change the way you see your own life?

Every person in this chapter is now watching. The author is about to tell his readers that this vast company of faithful men and women surrounds them like spectators in a stadium, cheering them on. And at the center of it all stands the one whose faith was greater than all of theirs combined: Jesus, the pioneer and perfecter of faith, who for the joy set before him endured the cross.

Turn the page.

10

THE RACE THAT LEADS HOME

In Homer's *The Iliad*, the greatest warriors of Greece are gathered on the plains of Troy. They fight not just for victory but for glory, for honor, for a name that will outlast their lives. What drives them forward through exhaustion and fear is the knowledge that others are watching. Their comrades in arms, the heroes who came before them, and the gods on Olympus are all fixed on the battle below. No warrior fights alone. Every blow struck, every wound endured, every moment of courage or cowardice is witnessed.

The author of Hebrews had something like that in mind when he wrote the opening of chapter 12. But he wasn't thinking about Greek warriors. He was thinking about Abel, Enoch, Noah, Abraham, Sarah, Moses, Rahab, and all the unnamed faithful he had just described in chapter 11. And he wasn't pointing to a battlefield. He was pointing to a racetrack.

In *Lilo & Stitch*, the word *ohana* means family, and "family means nobody gets left behind or forgotten." The film is about a broken family learning to hold on to each other against every force trying to tear them apart. By the end, even a destructive alien creature has been woven into the fabric of a family that refuses to let go. It's messy, imperfect, and beautiful. And in Hebrews 13, the author of this letter will close with a vision of community that sounds remarkably similar: love each other, welcome strangers, remember the imprisoned, honor your commitments, be content, follow your leaders, and never stop offering praise to God. Family means nobody gets left behind.

Chapters 12–13 are the finish line of Hebrews. Everything the author has been building toward, every warning, every promise, every theological argument about Jesus' priesthood, comes down to this: run the race, endure the discipline, approach the unshakable city, and live like the family of God you are.

THE RACE SET BEFORE US

"Therefore, since we are surrounded by such a great cloud of witnesses, let us throw off everything that hinders and the sin that so easily entangles. And let us run with perseverance the race marked out for us, fixing our eyes on Jesus, the pioneer and perfecter of faith."

Picture a stadium. The stands are packed, not with strangers but with every person from the faith chapter: Abel and his offering, Noah and his ark, Abraham leaving home, Sarah laughing in her tent, Moses walking away from Egypt, Rahab hiding the spies. They aren't just names in an old book. They are witnesses, people who lived the life of faith and are now watching from the stands as the readers of Hebrews take their turn on the track.

And the author says: run. Not casually. Not when you feel like it. Run with endurance, because this is a long race, and quitting is not an option. Strip off everything that slows you down, every distraction, every comfortable sin, every attachment to the world that wraps around your feet like a vine. Run light. Run focused. Run hard.

But here is the most important instruction of all: fix your eyes on Jesus. Not on the crowd. Not on the opposition. Not on your own tired legs. Look at Jesus, "the pioneer and perfecter of faith, who for the joy set before him endured the cross, scorning its shame, and sat down at the right hand of the throne of God."

Jesus ran this race first. He endured the worst opposition any human being has ever faced. The cross wasn't just painful; it was the most shameful form of execution the Roman Empire could inflict. And Jesus "scorned" that shame. He looked at the disgrace of the cross and decided it didn't matter, because on the other side of it was the joy of accomplishing his Father's will and taking his seat at God's right hand. The suffering was temporary. The triumph is forever.

The author says: when you're tired, when you feel like giving up, "consider him who endured such opposition from sinners, so that you will not grow weary and lose heart." Don't look at your problems. Look at Jesus.

THE DISCIPLINE OF A FATHER

But what about the suffering itself? Why does God let it happen? The author answers with a quotation from Proverbs: "My son, do not make light of the Lord's discipline, and do not lose heart when he rebukes you, because the Lord disciplines the one he loves, and he chastens everyone he accepts as his son."

This reframes everything. The hardship the readers are facing, the public insults, the loss of property, the social rejection, isn't random. It isn't punishment. It's discipline. And discipline is what a father gives a child he loves.

The author explains. Human fathers discipline their children for a short time, based on their own limited judgment. But God disciplines his children "for our good, in order that we may share in his holiness." The suffering that comes from living faithfully in a hostile world isn't meaningless. God is using it to shape his children into people who reflect his character. It's painful in the moment, but "later on, it produces a harvest of peace and righteousness for those who have been trained by it."

The point is both comforting and challenging. Comforting, because it means your suffering has a purpose and a loving Father behind it. Challenging, because the author warns that anyone who isn't experiencing this discipline "is not a true son or daughter at all." The absence of hardship isn't a sign that you're blessed. It might be a sign that you're not really in the family.

So the author says: "Strengthen your feeble arms and weak knees. Make level paths for your feet." In other words, get back up. Straighten out. Keep running. The discipline is making you stronger for the road ahead.

THE WARNING OF ESAU

Before showing his readers their glorious destination, the author pauses for one last warning. "See to it that no one falls short of the grace of God and that no bitter root grows up to cause trouble. See that no one is sexually immoral or godless like Esau, who for a single meal sold his inheritance rights as the oldest son."

Esau is the anti-hero of the entire letter. If chapter 11 was a hall of fame for faith, Esau is the cautionary tale hung on the exit door. He had the birthright, the promise of God passed down from Abraham through Isaac. It was his. And he traded it for a bowl of stew because he was hungry and couldn't be bothered to wait.

The author's point is devastating. Esau wasn't forced to give up his inheritance. He wasn't tricked. He just didn't care enough about eternal things to hold on to them when something temporary looked appealing. And when he later wanted the blessing back, "he was rejected. Even though he sought the blessing with tears, he could not change what he had done."

The readers of Hebrews are in danger of doing the same thing. Not by selling a birthright for stew, but by slowly letting go of Christ because the world is pressing hard and the faith feels costly. The author is saying: don't be an Esau. Don't trade the eternal for the temporary. Don't wake up one day and realize you've thrown away something you can never get back.

TWO MOUNTAINS

Now comes one of the most dramatic passages in the entire letter. The author places two mountains side by side and tells his readers which one they've come to.

The first is Sinai, though the author never calls it by name. He describes it the way someone in the crowd would have experienced it: fire, darkness, gloom, storm, a trumpet blast so terrifying that the people begged God to stop speaking, and the sight so awful that even Moses said, "I am trembling with fear." This is the mountain of God's holiness confronting human sin, and it offers no fellowship, no access, no comfort. It is judgment without mercy.

"But you," the author says, and everything changes. "You have come to Mount Zion, to the city of the living God, the heavenly Jerusalem. You have come to thousands upon thousands of angels in joyful assembly, to the church of the firstborn, whose names are written in heaven. You have come to God, the Judge of all, to the spirits of righteous people made perfect, to Jesus the mediator of a new covenant, and to the sprinkled blood that speaks a better word than the blood of Abel."

Where Sinai was terrifying, Zion is joyful. Where Sinai had no persons, only phenomena, Zion is filled with a community: angels celebrating, the faithful of all ages gathered, God himself present as judge and host, the righteous made perfect through Christ's sacrifice, and at the center of it all, Jesus, the mediator of the new covenant, whose blood doesn't cry for vengeance like Abel's but speaks forgiveness and welcome.

This is where the readers already stand through faith. This is the reality they enter every time they draw near to God through Christ. And this is the city they're running toward, the one that will last forever.

THE UNSHAKABLE KINGDOM

The author drives to his final theological point with the force of a hammer. God spoke at Sinai and shook the earth. But he has promised that one more time he will shake "not only the earth but also the heavens." Everything that can be shaken will be removed. Everything that cannot be shaken will remain.

And then this: "Therefore, since we are receiving a kingdom that cannot be shaken, let us be thankful, and so worship God acceptably with reverence and awe, for our God is a consuming fire."

The things of this world can be shaken and will be. Wealth, status, empires, even the physical universe itself will be removed. But the kingdom God gives his people through Christ is unshakable. It cannot be damaged, diminished, or destroyed. And if that is what you belong to, then nothing the world takes from you matters, because the one thing that lasts forever is the one thing that's already yours.

"Our God is a consuming fire." The letter that began with the radiance of God's glory closes with the fire of God's holiness. He is not safe in the way a stuffed animal is safe. He is safe the way a fortress is safe. You don't trifle with him. You worship him with reverence and awe, and you run the race knowing that the finish line is the threshold of his eternal presence.

A LIFE WORTHY OF THE RACE

Chapter 13 shifts from theology to practical instruction, but the connection to everything before it is seamless. If you belong to an unshakable kingdom and have a great High Priest who never stops interceding, then your ordinary, daily life should reflect those realities.

"Keep on loving one another as brothers and sisters." Show hospitality to strangers, because some who did this "entertained angels without knowing it," just as Abraham did. Remember prisoners as if you were chained beside them. Honor marriage. Be free from the love of money, and be content with what you have, "because God has said, 'Never will I leave you; never will I forsake you.'"

Remember your leaders who taught you the word of God. Consider how their lives ended and imitate their faith. And then, perhaps the most famous single verse in the entire letter: "Jesus Christ is the same yesterday and today and forever."

The leaders may change. The culture may shift. The pressure may increase. But the Jesus who saved you is the same one who walked out of the tomb, the same one who sat down at God's right hand, and the same one who will come again. He doesn't evolve, deteriorate, or expire. He is constant, and your faith can rest on something that never moves.

The author gives one final image drawn from the sacrificial system. On the Day of Atonement, the bodies of the sacrificial animals were burned "outside the camp." Jesus, too, "suffered outside the city gate to make the people holy through his own blood." And so the author calls his readers to follow Jesus "outside the camp, bearing the disgrace he bore. For here we do not have an enduring city, but we are looking for the city that is to come."

This is the pilgrim call that has echoed since chapter 11. Abraham left home looking for a city with foundations. The faithful died without receiving what was promised. And now the readers are told: you are pilgrims too. This world is not your home. Go to Jesus outside the camp, even if it costs you everything, because the city you're heading toward will never be shaken.

The letter's final instructions are acts of worship: "Through Jesus, let us continually offer to God a sacrifice of praise, the fruit of lips that openly profess his name. And do not forget to do good and to share with others, for with such sacrifices God is pleased."

Obey your leaders. Pray for one another. Grace be with you all.

WHAT THIS MEANS FOR US

First, you are not running alone. The cloud of witnesses isn't just a nice metaphor. It's a reminder that you belong to a story much bigger than yourself. Every person who has ever trusted God and kept going is part of your family. Their example strengthens you. Their faithfulness encourages yours.

Second, suffering is not a sign that God has forgotten you. It may be a sign that he's treating you as a beloved child. The discipline hurts, but it produces holiness and peace for those who are trained by it. Don't waste your suffering by resenting it. Let it shape you.

Third, don't trade the eternal for the temporary. Esau's mistake is available to anyone who stops caring about the things of God. The world will always offer something immediate and appealing in exchange for something invisible and eternal. The trade never, ever works in your favor.

Fourth, you have already arrived at Mount Zion. Through faith in Christ, you stand in the presence of angels, the gathered faithful, and God himself. The heavenly Jerusalem is not only your future destination. It is your present reality every time you draw near through Jesus. Live like someone who belongs there.

Fifth, Jesus Christ is the same yesterday, today, and forever. When everything else changes, he doesn't. Build your life on the one person who will never shift, fade, or fail.

TALKING POINTS

1. **The author tells his readers to "fix their eyes on Jesus."** What does that look like in everyday life? What are the things that most often pull your eyes away from him?

2. **The author says that the hardships believers face aren't random or meaningless. They are God's fatherly discipline, designed to strengthen his children and prepare them to share in his holiness.** How does understanding suffering as God's discipline change the way you experience hard times? Does it help to know that the pain has a purpose?

3. **Esau traded his birthright for a single meal.** What are the modern equivalents of that trade? What temporary things are most tempting to pursue at the cost of eternal ones?

4. **The contrast between Sinai and Zion is one of the most dramatic moments in Hebrews.** What does it mean that you have already "come to Mount Zion"? How should that shape the way you think about worship and prayer?

5. **"Jesus Christ is the same yesterday and today and forever."** Why is that statement so important for people going through change, uncertainty, or suffering?

The letter to the Hebrews began with the announcement that God has spoken his final word, and that word is his Son. It moved through a breathtaking portrait of who that Son is: the radiance of God's glory, the creator of the universe, the one who made purification for sins and sat down at the right hand of the Majesty in heaven. It showed him as a merciful High Priest who was tempted in every way yet without sin, who offered himself once for all, who entered the true sanctuary with his own blood, who mediates a better covenant, and who lives forever to intercede for his people.

And then it said: because of all this, run. Run with endurance. Run toward the city that cannot be shaken. Run looking at Jesus, who has already finished the race and is waiting for you at the end of it. You are surrounded by witnesses. You are loved by a Father who disciplines you for your good. You have an anchor for your soul, a priest who never stops, and a kingdom that will never fall.

The author of Hebrews wrote this letter to people who were tired, discouraged, and tempted to quit. His message to them, and to every generation that has read these words since, is simple and stunning: don't stop. The one who called you is faithful. The one who saved you is alive. The one who promised you a city is building it right now. And the one who endured the cross for the joy set before him is the same Jesus who will carry you all the way home.

www.ingramcontent.com/pod-product-compliance
Ingram Content Group UK Ltd.
Pitfield, Milton Keynes, MK11 3LW, UK
UKHW020420250726
13967UKWH00007B/2736

9 781971 767215